Behind
the
Door

Behind the Door

The Dark Truths and Untold Stories of the Cecil Hotel

Amy Price

WILLIAM MORROW

An Imprint of HarperCollins*Publishers*

HarperCollins books may be purchased for educational, business, or sales promotional use. For information, please email the Special Markets Department at SPsales@harpercollins.com.

FIRST EDITION

Library of Congress Cataloging-in-Publication Data has been applied for.

ISBN 978-0-06-325765-8

23 24 25 26 27 LBC 5 4 3 2 1

This book is dedicated to you, Pedro.

Two common and outstanding questions are, "How did I do it? Why did I stay?"

The simple answer is mostly because of you. There is little possibility that I would have survived for one day on the job if it hadn't been for you. Your approach to the world inspired me. It still does.

The language of friendship is not always words, but meanings. You mean a lot.

The years that I spent at the Cecil were some of the best and worst years of my life. The years came and went. Some better than others. Somehow, we managed, my friend.

You will always be an example of what it means when you meet someone who will change your whole life. You did just that. Our friendship came so naturally. I am so grateful for you, and I only smile when I think about you.

We worked together for a long time and the conditions were not always easy. Yet, somehow, we always managed to keep going. Courage is found in unlikely places and unreasonable circumstances.

I am confident that we will know each other for a long while. That is the beautiful part, my friend.

I consider our friendship a gift. The level of respect I have for you and the courage you gave me could not be measured in a lifetime.

I am humbly grateful to you. Thank you.

Contents

CONTENTS

Behind
the
Door

Introduction

Did you kill her?

You're a guilty bitch.

You belong in jail.

I thought you were great in the Netflix documentary.

These are some of the messages I've received recently. Unfortunately, since the documentary mentioned above was aired in 2021, I've become accustomed to strangers accusing me of murder and occasionally giving me a compliment. I've also become accustomed to death threats.

Being interviewed for a documentary (technically, it was a four-part docuseries) was one of the many things I didn't expect to happen when I took a three-day interior design gig at a hotel in downtown LA in 2007. I didn't expect to spend longer than three days there, and I definitely didn't expect to stay for a decade. When I was asked to participate in the Netflix series, I thought it was going to be about all the many colorful characters who passed through the Cecil Hotel. I didn't expect that it would center on the death of Elisa Lam. In fact, I was told that the goal was to not make it all about Elisa Lam, which, looking back, is an interesting detail.

If you're reading this book, then I assume it might be because you've seen *The Vanishing at the Cecil Hotel*. Maybe you've heard the Cecil referred to as "the deadliest hotel in Los Angeles," or "the most haunted." Maybe you know it as the place where the girl died in the water tank, or as the place where Richard Ramirez stayed in the '80s, or as the place where a lot of people have taken their own lives.

Here's what I can tell you: Whatever you might know about the Cecil is not enough to paint a full portrait. Beyond the sad news headlines, there are stories about actual people who lived actual lives. And, sure, a lot of those lives were marked by poverty and crime and bad behavior. Given the location of the hotel (right next to Skid Row), it was only natural that this would be true. But alongside the dismal stories, there are stories about hope, friendship, compassion, and love.

The most common question people ask me when I tell them I worked at the Cecil for ten years is, "Why did you stay?"

One answer is Pedro, the maintenance manager, who quickly became one of my best friends. He worked at the hotel for over thirty-five years, and actually still works there now, even though it's no longer a hotel; it's a living complex for formerly homeless people that is currently mostly vacant. From my first day on the job, it was clear that Pedro was the one who knew more about the Cecil than anyone. He was and is the hotel's unofficial historian. And to me, he's like family. There's no way I would have lasted at the job without him.

Pedro was the one who gave me my first tour of the hotel. Later, he was the first person I called when anything went wrong. He was the one who accompanied me to the roof with Elisa Lam's parents. It's now been years since we stopped working together, and he continues to be one of my closest confidants. Every month or so, I pick him up in front of what used to be the Cecil and we have lunch together. He calls me "Price," which is what my friends call me back home.

My relationship with Pedro probably speaks to one of the greatest gifts I got from working at the Cecil, which was exposure to people who weren't like me at all. I grew up in an extremely sheltered environment. I didn't know anything about what it meant to be an unauthorized immigrant in this country until I spent time with the employees at the hotel. I had no idea what it was like to sacrifice in that way. I guess I held the beliefs that everyone is created equal, and that if you called the cops, they would show up really fast like they do in the movies. Many of the incidents that occurred at the Cecil were things I'd only ever seen on TV.

This is probably the second answer to the question of why I stayed for so long: my own history. Sometimes I think my sheltered upbringing made me naïve to the real dangers happening around me at the Cecil. It also made me curious. Who were these people who seemed so unlike me? What did they care about? How had they arrived at this place?

What I want to do in this book is tell you the untold stories of all the Cecil tenants and guests who would probably otherwise remain anonymous. The title *Behind the Door* could be applied to every one of these people, but for me, it conjures one woman in particular, a woman who I didn't even know existed for a long time, because she never left her room. Her life, and the lives of many others I encountered at the Cecil, changed my understanding of the world and of myself in it, and I am forever grateful. Honestly, if the hotel hadn't closed, I'd probably still be there right now, running through the lobby in my heels, or sitting behind the enormous desk in my office, which was decorated with the opulence of a bygone era.

I often make the comparison between the Cecil and the *Titanic*. Both were built upon grandiose visions. And both sank. Looking back, I can see that the Cecil was sinking from the moment I stepped on board. At the time, though, I had grandiose visions of my own. Maybe those visions were another reason I stayed for ten years. I thought I could save the ship.

If you know anything about the history of the Cecil, you still might not understand why I didn't quit. Most people don't. My hope is that after you read this book, you will come to see why I couldn't leave. It would have felt like abandoning a family.

CHAPTER 1

A Fun Gig

In order to fully understand how foreign the landscape of downtown LA was to me, and how unprepared I was to oversee a hotel in which people were constantly dying, I need to tell you a little bit about where I'm from.

I grew up in a remote town called Clarkston, Michigan, on ten acres of land, and by "remote" I mean that school was an hour by bus from our house. In many ways, it was an idyllic childhood. We picked blueberries and had horses, llamas, roosters, and peacocks roaming freely as neighbors. I spent a lot of time in nature as a kid. I used to wander around our property, collecting rocks and washing them and sometimes fashioning them into imaginary diamond rings. Once, when I was eight or nine, I painted snail shells and tried to sell them at the end of our long driveway. These two memories are funny to think about now, because they perfectly foreshadow both my jewelry business and my interest in interior design, although I had no clue about that at the time. As a child, when I envisioned the future, I saw nothing specific. I wasn't one of those kids who was sure about what they wanted to become. I don't think I've ever had a solid plan in my entire life, to be honest. I've sort of just let the future unfold, which is perhaps another foreshadowing. If this weren't true about me, I probably wouldn't have ended up running a hotel in downtown LA.

In my household growing up, there wasn't only a love of great wide-open spaces. There was also a distaste for "city slickers," as my dad called them. He hated cities and couldn't understand why anyone would want to live in them. Every Christmas Eve, when we went to visit my grandpa in Detroit, my sister and I were told not to look out the car windows because whatever was happening out there was too dangerous for children to see. So, of course, as a young kid, I came to believe that cities were scary and bad.

I also believed that my family was happy as a kid—until one day when I was twelve, my mother, without warning, picked my sister and me up and told us she was leaving our father and moving us to our grandmother's house in a suburb called Royal Oak. I remember writing about it in my Hello Kitty diary and misspelling "divorce." Compared to Clarkston, Royal Oak seemed prettier and city-like, even though it wasn't at all. At first, I was daunted, but eventually I acclimated.

Three years later, when I was fifteen years old, we moved again, this time to Birmingham, Michigan, to live in a wealthier area. On the outside, our lives appeared to be stable. Our house was nice, our pool was nice, our new town was nice. But it wasn't an easy time. My parents were still fighting a custody battle. Not wanting to hurt either of their feelings, I told them each privately that I wanted to live with them, and then, when I was forced to make a choice in court, I chose my mom. It was stressful, and as a result, I stopped eating and started cutting myself and pulling out my own hair in the bathroom. I also started skipping school. This was the only rebellion my mother noticed and it really upset her.

One day, she asked me why I'd stopped going to class. "Are you an alcoholic?" she wanted to know. "Are you a drug addict?"

And for whatever reason—I still don't completely understand why I did this, because I wasn't drinking or doing drugs—I said yes. I think that subconsciously I just wanted to get away from home. Looking back on it today, I desperately wanted to escape the stress of being home.

Within a few hours, my mom had checked me into a drug rehab center, where I would stay for six blissful weeks. I felt comfortable there, and safe, and it was a nice reprieve from my mother's anger. I won't go too far into the details here, because my own trauma is not the point of this book, but I do think it's important to know that many of my formative experiences were traumatic, and this was probably another reason why I stayed at the Cecil for as long as I did. It might have also been a reason why I had such compassion for most of the tenants there, who'd been through their own traumas.

Some people become hardened when they grow up in a less-than-nurturing environment, but for me, it produced the opposite result. It made me into a nurturer. Ever since I was a kid, I've been drawn to helping the people around me, sometimes to a fault—which is the perfect segue to Teddy, my rehab boyfriend.

Teddy was gorgeous, charismatic, and flawed, and from the moment I met him, I wanted to save him. After rehab (where I not only pretended to be a drug addict for six weeks, but also quickly rose to the position of team leader), Teddy and I continued dating, and I continued thinking that I could rescue him from his addictions. After he left our high school for military school in Virginia, we kept in touch. I had no idea when I was a teenager how Teddy would end up impacting my life, and how devastating it would be.

The idea to go to a community college in East Lansing felt sort of like an afterthought. Getting a college degree wasn't highly expected from me. My sister had always been viewed as the "smart one." I was always just getting by. My sister graduated from the University of Michigan in less than four years. I didn't really care about school at the time, nor did I think I was good at it, because I'd done so poorly in high school.

I think what I enjoyed most about East Lansing was that it wasn't home. I had my own apartment, freedom, and no interest in going to class—which meant that I flunked out in the first year. After that, my mom told me to come home and get a job. So, feeling like a failure, I returned to Birmingham and started working at Chili's.

My ascension through the ranks at Chili's was similar to me quickly becoming the team leader at the rehab. It's also exactly what I did at the Cecil, which we'll get to shortly. I've been successful at every job I've ever had because I'm dedicated, trustworthy, and diligent. I can cross everything off a list, and quickly. Sometimes even I am shocked by how much I can accomplish in a day. If I'm running at full speed, I can handle a lot of work. And I can handle a lot of stress. It's also apparently in my nature to assume a large amount of responsibility, even if it hasn't been assigned to me, which is why, at nineteen years old, I was promoted to a trainer position at Chili's, and then to a bartender position. In Michigan it was legal to be a bartender if you were over eighteen.

On a good night at Chili's, I made $120, which was a ton of money to me at the time. It was also enough for me to afford my own apartment. Within a few months of moving home, I'd moved out. For a while, I felt happy about my job and my independence. But then, as more time passed, I started to realize that a future at Chili's wasn't going to be enough for me. So I decided to return to school. I asked my mom if I could move back in while I continued my studies. After a couple of weeks of thinking about it, she offered to pay for college instead. She mentioned a college in Northern Michigan, about four hours away. I was accepted and for the first time in my life I learned that I had any brains at all when I got straight As. When I told my mom, she said she'd only expected Cs.

For the next few years, I bounced around the state, going from college to college while working odd jobs when I wasn't in class. One of those jobs was at the Detroit Auto Show, which took place every January. There, I followed my usual workplace trajectory of assuming a lot of responsibility and being rewarded for it. I started as a seasonal employee during a break at my mother's house between colleges, and by the time I'd finished my senior year at Eastern Michigan University, I was a full-time employee. At work, unlike at school, I felt confident and capable. I was happy to show up early and stay late. I loved everything about it.

Shortly after I got the job at the auto show, an event marketing company in California called George P. Johnson offered me a position. I remember telling my mother that I didn't want it. Why leave the wonderful job I already had in Michigan? I loved my friends. I loved my job. Why would I want to move to California?

If you watched the docuseries, you might remember that I called my mother before I called the police after Elisa Lam's body was found. That is because she was and still is my number one sounding board. At twenty-five, when I told her about the job opportunity in California, she said I absolutely needed to leave.

"Don't you want to do something different? What are you going to do? Hang out in the same place and at the same job your whole life?"

No, I didn't necessarily want to do anything different, but I did it anyway. I packed my Honda Accord EX up to the gills. In the driveway, my mother gave me some oversimplified directions. "Go west, Amy. If you feel confused, pull over and make sure you're going west." Thanks, Mom!

Of course, this was pre-smartphones, so driving through the country felt like much more of a task than it does today. But I managed to get there in one piece. I'd been to California twice before (once for the interview at George P. Johnson and once on a short trip with a friend), but I knew nothing about how to live there. I spent my very first night at a friend's boyfriend's house in Camarillo, and the next day, I drove to Hollywood. Or I tried to drive to Hollywood, but then I realized I didn't know where it was. I pulled into a gas station and asked the cashier, "Do you know how to get to Hollywood?" The cashier was unfriendly and unhelpful. It was a culture shock to me. In Michigan, people hurried to help you, especially at gas stations. In California, people were kind of rude.

I ended up moving into an apartment with a couple of college friends in the Hollywood Hills. Meanwhile, my job was in Torrance.

For those of you who aren't familiar with LA geography, this is a terrible commute. Which is why within a year, I moved to Hermosa Beach. This is where I really started to feel settled in my California life. Hermosa Beach, unlike LA, is small and quaint. I found a cute beach shack with a roommate and a bunch of new women friends. I felt great. During the days I worked hard, and at night my new friends and I would sit outside and drink cheap wine, smoke endless cigarettes, and talk.

One of those new friends was a woman named Tori, who was very pretty, always broke, and smoked Marlboro Ultra Lights. Another was a Camel Lights smoker named Cindy. Cindy and I became especially close. She had pursued her creative passion and was working as an online college professor and writer at the time, which I admired, because I had creative dreams of my own. It was when I lived in Hermosa Beach that I started my jewelry business. During my free time, I'd go collect all the necessary materials and make necklaces and bracelets and earrings. At first, I named the company after my great-grandmother Ruth Burgess. Looking back, I can see that I did that because I was afraid of putting my own name on my work. I wanted to be an artist, but I was also scared to be an artist. It would take me twenty more years to work up the courage to rename my business Amy Price Jewelry.

What Cindy and I shared, besides a love of Charles Shaw wine and smoking (Marlboro Lights were my poison, in case you were wondering), was an interest in interior design. To me, decorating a space is a lot like designing a piece of jewelry. It uses the same part of the brain. When Cindy and I got together, we often geeked out on art, home furnishings, paint color choices, and anything else that fed our creative minds.

Soon after I met Cindy, she married her then-boyfriend, Steve, who was a minor character in my life in the beginning. I didn't know much about Steve except that he worked in the hotel business and had some children from a previous marriage. He was also twelve years older than Cindy, which, at the time, seemed like a big age difference. Their wedding reception took place at the Belamar in Manhattan Beach, which is a gorgeous hotel that Steve had helped to revamp. He worked as a hotel rehabber, which could mean a great number of things, depending on what the property needed. Sometimes he was redesigning lobbies and rooms, and other times he was gutting a place completely. His title was very succinctly expressed on his personalized license plate: HOTELMD.

Years went by in Hermosa Beach, and things mostly stayed the same. I continued to make jewelry in my free time, and I started selling it at art shows on the weekends. I got closer to Cindy and Steve, and I was incredibly grateful to them, too, because they were so supportive of my business. Once, Cindy let me borrow her Porsche to take to a show because it was bigger than my car. I considered them to be a cool, successful couple, and I was just so happy that they'd entered my life.

During the weekdays, I kept showing up for work at George P. Johnson. Then, six years into my California life, I took a new position, this time as a salesperson at an automotive marketing company. The switch included a big pay raise and a ridiculous amount of travel. Suddenly, I wasn't managing my own schedule anymore. I was just being told things like, "You're in Wichita tomorrow," and then I had no choice but to go to Wichita.

In short, the new job was brutal. I worked eighteen-hour days, and my life was out of balance. This was a stark contrast to the way my long-distance boyfriend was living. Yes, I had a long-distance boyfriend, Carter, who I'd met in high school and who still lived in Michigan, so most of our relationship took place over the phone. Carter, unlike me, had a trust fund and therefore not a whole lot of motivation to work. He also lacked a fire in his belly. While I may have envied what appeared to be Carter's easier life in some ways, I was mostly grateful for his comfort. Talking to him aways made me feel better, and hopeful about the future, too.

After I got a new job that would require me to move to Philadelphia, he agreed to move there with me. But when I started talking about how we needed to look for housing, Carter backed out. And after that, I decided that I would, too. I didn't want to move to Philadelphia alone. Right before I was about to tell the new company I wouldn't be coming, the luckiest thing happened: I was laid off.

It felt like the message I was receiving from the universe was to take a little break, so that's what I did. I started collecting unemployment, which was enough to cover my cheap rent. I also started collecting sand dollars off the beach, where I'd take daily walks. It was a reflective time, and a necessary one. It was the first time I'd paused since leaving Michigan. I remember when I found my first sand dollar, I was surprised. There were sand dollars in California? What else had I been missing? I was also asking some bigger questions about what I wanted to do with my life. I was good at sales, but did I care about sales? I was in no rush to figure anything out. I was happy to take a break. I felt at peace. I was also blissfully single. At some point after our failed Philadelphia plans, Carter made a plan to propose to me. I already knew I'd say no. Our relationship ended shortly after that.

During this period of reflection, I read Julia Cameron's *The*

Artist's Way, which changed my point of view on art-making. I felt enlivened after I read it, and I understood for the first time that the reason I hadn't pursued a creative path was because I was scared of failure. I told Cindy about how the twelve-week course had enhanced my life, and she ended up taking it, too, and after that the book became another frequent topic of conversation during our hangouts.

One night, about six months into my peaceful period of unemployment, the usual group of women was hanging out at night on my patio drinking Charles Shaw and possibly nibbling on one of those hummus trios from Trader Joe's. Cindy was there, and so was Tori, and I'm sure we were talking about *The Artist's Way*, and probably also *The Bachelor*, which we all watched religiously back then. At some point in the conversation, Cindy mentioned offhandedly that Steve had a new hotel in downtown LA and that he needed help redesigning one of the rooms to replicate a Best Western room so that it could be used as a model for investors. During my time at the Cecil, there were many, many visions for how it would succeed, and at this point, becoming a Best Western was the answer.

Cindy said the job wouldn't be a big deal. "Only three days," she said. "They'll give you a photo of a Best Western, and you'll just copy it."

I thought it sounded like a fun gig. I was young and healthy and happy to drive around town looking for furnishings that matched the ones in the photo we'd be given. And I was jobless. What else did I have to do? Tori said she wanted in, too. Since she was always broke, she needed the money.

When Steve came to pick Cindy up that night (he always dropped her off and picked her up), he seemed pleased that we'd agreed to do the job and told us to show up at the Cecil Hotel the following day. It all seemed fairly straightforward. We'd design one room and be done three days later. I had no idea how saying yes to this random gig would alter the course of my life.

CHAPTER 2

A Sort of Impressive Shithole

I'd never heard of the Cecil Hotel, and the only thing I knew about downtown LA was that it was a shithole.

I also knew that the common response to saying "Downtown LA is a shithole" was something about hope and renewal and change. I suppose the correct term that might encapsulate all of these would be "gentrification." The myth of how cleanliness and order would erase Skid Row was alive and well even back then.

The Cecil Hotel was located on Main Street, which used to be a part of Skid Row, but no longer was. I remember this being a selling point in the beginning. "And it's no longer on Skid Row." What had happened was that Skid Row had been pushed back a block. So no, the hotel was no longer part of Skid Row. It was just next to it.

I didn't see Skid Row on the first day. What I remember about driving downtown was that all the one-way streets were confusing and full of potholes. Steve had told me to park behind the hotel, in the lot, and to get there I had to drive down a creepy, dark alley. Later, after a few years went by, I would become so used to seeing drug use and prostitution in this alley that the sight of it lost its shock value. Like many of the sketchy things that happened at the Cecil, it was both disturbing and commonplace.

After I parked, I looked up at the hotel. I was impressed by how enormous it was, and sort of irked, too, because it was obviously run-down. Maybe I was spoiled, as I was a regular at the Marriott (I was a Platinum member, too), but I didn't think this was a premium place to stay. The exterior of the Cecil also had an ominous air, which I dismissed as I looked for Steve.

He guided me from the lot to the front entrance. If I had to guess, he was probably talking about how great downtown was going to become very soon during the short walk, and I was probably thinking about how funny it was that I'd dressed up to walk around scary downtown. I'm sure I was wearing something from J.Crew, something from Banana Republic, heels, my hair in curls, and, of course, my own jewelry. Part of how I take a job seriously is that I dress up for it. Also, I just like dressing up. My friends call me "fancy Amy." If I'm actually going somewhere fancy, then it makes sense. At the Cecil, I definitely stuck out.

The first time I walked into the lobby, I was taken aback by how grand it seemed. This was possibly all due to sheer size. It was huge, and some of the décor, like the wide marble columns and the chandelier, was opulent and clearly very expensive. I didn't quite put this together at the time, but the reason the nice chandelier wasn't removed was because it was too high up to steal. That the lobby had no furniture in it should have been a red flag about what type of clientele the Cecil attracted, and the laundry area, which was visible from the lobby, should have been a sign of the confused identity of the place, which catered to both hotel guests and long-term tenants. And then, too, there were the tenants themselves, walking through the lobby or waiting for their clothes to dry. My general impression was that these people did not seem to be thriving, but I didn't think that was any of my business at the time. I was doing a three-day job, and then I'd be gone.

Soon after we entered the lobby, Steve introduced me to Pedro. "Pedro will give you a tour," he said, although he might have accidentally called Pedro "Pablo," which he often did. From the very first second I met Pedro, I just liked him. He seemed sweet and endearing, and his smile put me at ease.

It might have been during that very first tour that Pedro told me he'd been working at the hotel since 1984, when the environment downtown was even rougher than it was when I arrived in 2007. Later, I would learn that Pedro had arrived in the States with no ID. He said back then it was easy to just walk back and forth across the Mexican border without a problem. He eventually got a job as a janitor at the Cecil and was later promoted to the role of maintenance manager. Over the years, he'd seen countless employees come and go. This is what made him the hotel's unofficial historian. He'd been there longer than anyone else.

After we left the lobby, the hotel stopped looking so grand. The carpet in the guest rooms was sticky and disgusting like the carpets in casinos. The communal shower stalls didn't even have curtains on them. They just had liners. And there were so many rooms. I don't know why this was a surprise to me, because in large print on the side of the hotel was a sign advertising seven hundred rooms, but for some reason, seeing all those doors made it seem more real. (I would later learn that the hotel had six hundred rooms, so I'm not sure why that sign said seven hundred.) More surprisingly, the doors all had multiple locks on them, because the Cecil was still operating on a key system as opposed to a key-card system. This meant that somebody could leave with the keys and then sneak back in later and have access to their old room. When that happened, a new lock would be added to the door.

The other thing about the doors was that many of them were dented. When I asked Pedro why, he explained it like this: "People's fists."

What? People's fists? I knew that wasn't a great answer, but somehow I assumed that whatever fighting had happened at the hotel belonged firmly in the past and would stay there. Certainly, no one in the future would be punching a door.

It was a few days later that I would learn about how consistently deaths occurred at the hotel. Pedro and I were standing in the elevator together. He always wore a walkie-talkie at that time, and the jibber jabber between the front desk and housekeeping was audible. I very distinctly heard the words, "Somebody died." I was shocked. *Died?* Yes, died, Pedro said, and then he told me not to worry. It happened all the time.

"What?" I was even more shocked.

When we got off the elevator, he pointed at a room and said, "Somebody died in there, too." He pointed to another room. "And in there."

"How many people have died at this hotel?" I asked.

And Pedro, with his dark sense of humor, said, "A lot."

Pedro's dry sense of humor and his calm around this subject were bizarre to me at first. They were also kind of comforting. If

Pedro wasn't freaking out, then there was no reason for me to, either. I'm sure I was also holding on to the delusion that downtown LA was on the brink of change, which meant that soon, fewer people would be dropping dead, just like fewer people would be punching doors. This was naïve of me, and it would turn out to be very incorrect. During the ten years I worked at the Cecil, about eighty people died.

The hotel, I would later learn, had a long history of death. In 1924, when it opened, it was grand and beautiful and full of promise. And then the Depression hit in 1929. Did that have anything to do with the suicide that happened in 1931? Or the one that followed, in 1934, when a woman took a razor to her throat? Later, in 1962, a woman jumped out a window and landed on a man who was walking down the street. They both died instantly. In 1964, a woman was brutally raped and killed in the hotel in the middle of the day. In the 1980s, the environment became even more grizzly. Allegedly, serial killer Richard Ramirez, otherwise known as the Night Stalker, stayed at the Cecil. In the Netflix documentary, one interviewee called it the place where "serial killers went to let their hair down."

Over the course of the next few days, as Pedro and I walked around the hotel together, he would continue to tell me stories about death. I found each detail upsetting, which is probably why I remember them so well. The first story was about a man who'd been discovered after a long period of being dead. He was found in his room, lying on his back in the middle of the floor. When the coroner came to collect his body, they picked him up—and his head fell apart in their hands. The writhing maggots were a sign of how long the body had been there. Pedro told me this story in the very room in which it had taken place. He pointed at the center of the floor and said, "Right there."

Pedro told me another story in one of the rooms that we would later turn into the community space for Stay, which is what we eventually renamed a section of the Cecil. (I'll come back to this soon.) It was made up of two rooms, which, combined, offered just enough square footage for a foosball table, comfortable seating, and a computer area. Pedro, again, told me the horrific story as we stood in the place where it had happened. A fight broke out between two gay lovers, he explained, and things got bloody. One man stabbed the other multiple times. Pedro was taken in for questioning on that one, which seemed funny to me. Even though I didn't know him well yet, it was clear that he wasn't capable of hurting a fly.

After I'd heard these stories, it was hard not to think about them as I walked around the hotel. As I redesigned the community room, the bloody lover would pop into my mind, and whenever I walked by the room in which the man had been lying dead for a long period, I'd think of maggots. Pedro's stories about death were haunting, but they were also far removed from my experience. I didn't actually see any blood or maggots or dead bodies. These details were historical. If not for the stench of the Cecil, which matched the doom of death on the most visceral level, I probably could have cast Pedro's tales aside more efficiently.

Also, I don't think I process fear like most other people do. Having spent my early life in idyllic rural Michigan, I was accustomed to safety. I thought the world was essentially a good place where people made strong decisions. Instead of being petrified by the apparent danger of the Cecil, I thought it was kind of exciting.

My most vivid memory of that first tour is the smell. I can only describe it as something like hot urine, bad breath, and cigarette smoke mixed together. The air was thick and putrid. When I asked Pedro why it smelled so bad, he said, "It's because people don't shower." I never understood this answer. If I didn't shower for a week, I would not smell like the Cecil did. It was rank. I would soon learn that in the summer, it was even worse, because the hotel had no air-conditioning. (It didn't have central heat, either.)

The floors on which the tenants lived (two and three) were particularly foul-smelling. The floors on which there were no tenants were better, but not perfect. There was actually an incentive program before I arrived at the Cecil to contain the tenants (there were eighty or ninety of them when I arrived) on floors two and three. This was partly because of the smell, not to mention the tenants themselves, many of whom were mentally ill and sometimes exhibited strange and inappropriate behavior. The idea was that if they were all together on two floors, then the remaining floors could be used for other populations that would bring in more money.

On the sixth floor, which contained only hotel rooms and smelled okay, Pedro showed me the room I'd be redesigning, which was technically two Cecil rooms. The wall between them had been removed. The average size of a Cecil room was 120 square feet, which is incredibly small—and which is why most of the rooms (all but roughly seven on each floor) didn't have toilets or showers. Whoever stayed in these rooms was required to use the shared toilets at the end of the hall. (This seemingly tiny detail was one of the hotel's biggest problems, and perhaps a main contributing factor to its demise.) When the wall was knocked down between two Cecil rooms, it gave the impression that it was a suite, with a main room and an adjoining room. Or at least this is what the owners hoped the Best Western investors would see.

The way it was explained to me in the beginning was that eventually, the entire place would become a Best Western and the tenants would be moving out. "Soon, this will all be a lot nicer" was the gist of the spiel. It was the same spiel people liked to give about downtown LA. What I had absolutely no understanding of on day one was how tenants' legal rights would inhibit this plan.

Pedro and I returned downstairs, where I learned that a bulletproof glass shield had just been removed from the front desk. The employees were terrified after that, they told me, because they'd become so accustomed to the protection. And they had good reason to be, if you glanced at the reports filed by the front desk and security guards. Here's an example:

> At around 10am many of us received calls from different guests stating that someone was screaming and it seemed like domestic violence. One houseman reported it as well. Samantha called the room and the male guest answered the phone. Samantha asked if everything was okay. He didn't respond but the female guest got on the phone and said no. Later, within five to seven minutes, someone pressed the elevator emergency button. Samantha saw a male guest pick up the female guest and carry her out of the elevator. I then saw him pick her up by the feet and drag her into the lobby.
>
> I immediately dialed 911. Security had already called LAPD. The male guest kept dragging the victim out of the lobby but stopped before the exit. LAPD entered and arrested him. The female guest was still laying on the floor.

Here is another note left at the front desk:

At approximately 7:15am, an anonymous caller called the front
desk reporting a person with a knife in the alley behind the hotel.
Security reported that there was no one with a knife, but there was
a male laying in the alley. The male appeared to be dead since he
was not moving and was bleeding from his head.

Paramedics arrived minutes after and the LAFD declared the
man to be dead on arrival. They identified him as hotel guest
Travis Schwartz, who is registered to room 1440. He was due to
check out this morning.

Around 9:45am, the coroner arrived to retrieve the body and
all the belongings in room 1440. Since we did not retrieve the
room key from Mr. Schwartz, I called a houseman to change the
lock.

I also learned that a baby had been born behind the front desk,
which seemed unbelievable. I clocked these details with more curiosity than fear. The Cecil was definitely the most interesting place
I'd ever worked.

The tour lasted about an hour, and then Pedro dropped me off at
the conference room, where Steve was working on his laptop. He presented me with the photo I was supposed to replicate, which looked
exactly how you would expect a Best Western room to look, and I
spent the next three days with Tori driving around LA in search of
matching items.

I rented a U-Haul on my credit card and paid for everything myself with the understanding that I'd be reimbursed. I didn't think this
was weird at the time, although maybe I should have. I copied every

single detail of that Best Western room to the absolute best of my ability. I found the perfect alarm clock. I had curtains custom-sewn. Since there was no bathroom, we did a mock bathroom instead.

Pedro and a group of employees helped us load and unload the U-Haul, although by "us," I'm really just referring to myself. I mean this in the most loving way, but Tori was deadweight on my canoe. She literally fell asleep in the truck while I was running around choosing things because she'd taken a Tylenol PM by mistake to cure her hangover.

From the beginning, I was given a lot of responsibility and independence, and I rose to the occasion. The Best Western–esque room turned out magnificently. In my personal opinion, it had an ugly color scheme, but that was beside the point. I had done what I'd been asked to do. And Steve was very happy. He had never seen anyone work so hard—and he didn't want to let me go.

CHAPTER 3

Such Excitement

The plan unfolded organically.

The Best Western deal was put on pause, and in the meantime, Steve was given the freedom to explore a different vision. He hired me to stay on as a designer, along with Cindy, who'd decided she wanted to help. This time, it wouldn't be a matter of just copying a photo. We would be given creative license to design the rooms on floors four, five, and six however we wanted. The goal was to revamp just this small section and rebrand it as a separate hotel. What was below it (floors two and three) would continue to belong to the tenants of the Cecil, and all the floors above it would belong to its short-term guests.

Let me stop here and explain why the Best Western deal was put on pause, because this is important. A quiet lawsuit between the owners of the hotel and the broker who'd sold it to them was unfolding behind the scenes. The owners, who'd bought the place right before I arrived in 2007, claimed that the broker had never told them that the Cecil was operating as a residential hotel. The broker disputed this. He claimed that he had honestly disclosed the way in which the Cecil was functioning. I am unsure how the broker wouldn't have been aware of the politics, but apparently that was the claim.

How could the owners not have known that there were tenants at the Cecil? Because they signed up for an investment and didn't have plans to be involved with the day-to-day activities at the hotel. They were investors, not hotel enthusiasts. Also, they lived in different cities and weren't that familiar with the area. Like all the owners before them, what they saw was the amazing potential of the Cecil as a fully functioning hotel, possibly even a luxurious one. From a purely visual perspective, it seemed possible. Later, a large part of my job at the Cecil would be giving tours to potential investors. I'd take people up to the roof and point to the Pacific Electric Building and say, "*Batman* was filmed over there." I'd point to the rooftop swimming pools around us, and it was easy for investors to envision a future in which the Cecil would also have a rooftop pool. All of them thought, as I did in the beginning, that the hotel could be saved.

As it stood, most of the Cecil's income was derived from tenants' rents, and those were very cheap. Some people were paying $200 a week and some $400 a month. The longer they'd been there, the less they paid, and many tenants had moved in thirty or forty years earlier. This meant that financially, the Cecil was hovering just above the red. By sectioning off 138 rooms and raising the price, Steve hoped that the property would start making a greater profit.

Before I tell you about how we redesigned those 138 rooms, let me paint a more specific picture of what the place was like when I got there. In addition to the laundry room in the lobby, the dents in the doors, and the putrid smells, there were the guests, who often checked in with trash bags instead of suitcases. On the first of the month, which was when many of our clientele received government-issued checks, the lobby was flooded with people who were often otherwise homeless. They'd stay at the hotel for a night or two to take a shower and clean up, and then they'd leave again. Most guests paid in cash, and we weren't extremely strict on IDs. Which made the Cecil especially attractive to people who didn't have valid IDs and/or who wanted to remain anonymous. Who doesn't have an ID? Who wants to remain anonymous? Generally speaking, it is the people who exist in the shadows of society. More specifically, it is unauthorized immigrants, drug dealers, pedophiles, homeless people, and others who are not exactly doing that well, to put it lightly. This was the population to which the Cecil catered. Basically, it was the place you went when you had nowhere else to go.

Along with the short-term guests, there were the long-term residents of the hotel. These populations had a lot in common—except for stability. The guests were transient, whereas the residents were fixtures so permanent that it was as if they'd been built into the foundation. When I arrived, there were about eighty residents, all of whom had been living at the hotel for years, and very few of whom would leave of their own accord during the decade that I worked there. When a residential room freed up, it was generally because the resident had died or been incentivized or had relocated to a hospital because of illness. If our goal was to one day become a proper hotel, then we couldn't have people paying monthly. We would need only short-term guests, and ideally, they would be people who checked in with suitcases rather than trash bags. In order to make a profit, we would have to start attracting travelers who were willing to pay a higher rate—and share bathrooms.

And so the idea for a hostel was born. We would redesign the rooms on floors four, five, and six in a way that would appeal to young travelers on a budget, and we would give this section of the hotel a new name: Stay. It seemed like a great plan. Or maybe it seemed like the only plan. The layout of the hotel didn't leave us a lot of options. As I mentioned earlier, the issue of the communal bathrooms was a kiss of death for the Cecil in terms of it ever becoming a real moneymaker. The other kiss of death was the shared elevator bank. Both of these architectural choices were huge obstacles, because if we ever wanted to change them, it would be extremely complicated, not to mention insanely expensive. And we had very little money. So we were going to have to make do with the existing layout—and with the existing population at the Cecil.

How was a young traveler on a budget going to feel when they walked into the lobby and saw people who looked kind of homeless checking in with trash bags instead of suitcases? And what were they going to think of sharing an elevator with these people, who often didn't smell very good?

We had no tangible solution for the elevator problem, but we did come up with a solution for the lobby. On either side of the Cecil entrance, there were retail spaces that the hotel owned. One was a shady minimart that had closed down. The other was a former lens shop. If you walked through the lens shop, there was a staircase at the back that led up to what would become the area where Stay joined the Cecil by the elevator banks. All we had to do was take down a small wall in order to create that passageway, which wasn't a big deal.

Creating a separate lobby for Stay seemed like a great workaround. The only issue was that it wouldn't have an elevator accessible. Guests would have to climb stairs with their luggage to get to the elevator banks. This meant that later, when somebody who was disabled arrived, we would have to ask them to go through the Cecil lobby.

The more exposure I got to the tenants at the Cecil, the more worried I became about our Stay guests sharing space with them. A few weeks into my new gig, I walked over to Rite Aid to grab a snack. On my way back to the hotel, I noticed that a man was walking behind me. His face was decorated in lipstick (maybe in a tribal pattern?), and there was a cigarette dangling from his mouth. Was he following me or was I imagining things? I wasn't sure—and then he started to chase me while shouting. I was a little bit scared, and very glad when I made it back to the hotel safely.

And then the man walked in.

He was one of our tenants.

Later, I'd learn his name was Sam.

At the start, I was afraid of Sam, but after a while, we formed a close bond. He was an unforgettable man, and even now, I think of him often. Everything was just a little bit off about Sam. As I mentioned earlier, he liked to draw on his face with lipstick, and sometimes he used markers and makeup, too. Sam was colorful both in appearance and character. Also, he was always drunk.

Some of my fondest—and most curious—memories of Sam took place in front of Marty, the coffee shop located between Stay and Cecil, where he liked to sit and tell me stories. I just loved listening to him. Even though a lot of what he said didn't make that much sense, I found him to be very entertaining. One thing he spoke of often were "giggle weeds." According to Sam, giggle weeds were located in

New Jersey, where he was originally from, and the people who lived inside the weeds would grab you as you walked by. I'll stop with the details there, because they're beyond nonsensical, but hopefully this illustrates how Sam's brain worked.

Sam's actions were as odd as his words. He once claimed to have sent Ellen DeGeneres a bunch of maxi pads with ketchup on them (I'm not sure why he chose Ellen DeGeneres or what his intended messaging was), and another time, he ordered me multiple subscriptions to magazines. He just wrote my name on the subscription cards that you find inside magazines and added the Cecil's address. When they arrived at the hotel, he admitted to having ordered them, but he never explained why.

Sam also claimed to be afflicted with AIDS, cancer, and a variety of other diseases that I can no longer remember. It was always hard to tell how much of what he said was true and how much of it was false, but I was inclined to believe that Sam was sick in some way. His lifestyle was so unhealthy. At some point, he lost all his teeth. At another point, he tested positive for tuberculosis.

Sam shared a room at the Cecil with his lover, Joe. Both men were in their sixties and, according to the amount of rent they paid, hadn't lived there long. (Rent price was usually the first thing I looked at when I was trying to figure out how long a tenant had been at the Cecil. As a general rule of thumb, the people who paid the lowest rents had been there the longest.) Joe and Sam paid a sizable amount, much more than many of the other tenants. I wasn't sure how they afforded their rent, but they always paid on time.

Joe, unlike Sam, was a mysterious man to me, and much less friendly. I never formed a bond with him. I knew that he had at least one child, a son, who would come visit him sometimes. And

I knew that there were rumors circling around that Joe beat Sam at night. Other tenants reported that they could hear Sam crying in their room. After I heard this, I asked Sam if he felt safe, and he said yes. There wasn't much more I could do than ask.

Sam, as I mentioned before, loved to sit outside the coffee shop and tell stories while drinking his liquor out of Styrofoam cups. People, including me, would congregate out there to listen to him. Joe was often outside, too, but he was usually quiet. He might have been drinking, but I never saw him drunk. He appeared to be very composed, whereas Sam had drawings all over his face and sometimes straws sticking out of his ears. Joe wore responsible jeans and polos while Sam wore the wackiest outfits. For all these reasons, their relationship never made sense to me.

In many buildings, fumigators are hired to keep cockroach and other infestations at bay. Well, this was the intention at the Cecil, too. We had a fumigator named Juan who came every month, and although he definitely did his job, he wasn't exactly making progress. Juan's purpose was to get rid of infestations for our tenants, but our tenants were the main source of the infestations. Many of them left food out and did not keep their rooms in good condition. It was a bad loop.

Every month, our tenants received a notification that their rooms would be sprayed. The protocol was that if they weren't home, then Juan was allowed to open their doors. One day, Juan opened Sam and Joe's door to find Sam curled up next to Joe's dead body in their bed. Based on the state of Joe's body, it was clear that he'd been dead for a few days. We immediately reported the death, and the police were called. I remember escorting them to Sam and Joe's room on the third floor.

At first, the cops seemed to think the Sam might have been responsible for Joe's death. I remember waiting outside the room while they questioned him. And then they questioned me about Sam. I told them there was absolutely no way Sam was a murderer. He was just strange. Also, Joe appeared to have had a heart attack. How could Sam have been responsible for that? Even if he possessed the ability to kill, he was physically too weak to accomplish a suffocation, or any other kind of murder. The cops eventually let their theory go, and Joe's body was removed from the building. I remember thinking about how bizarre it was that Joe had died before Sam, because he seemed like the healthy one.

After Joe's death, Sam didn't do well on his own. He stopped showering, maybe almost completely. He smelled horrible all the time and he hung out in the lobby more often, exhibiting disruptive and sometimes reckless behavior. Whoever was working the front desk often encouraged Sam to go back up to his room when that happened, and the security guard on duty did the same thing. When Sam wasn't being disruptive, though, he was a great source of entertainment for all the people who worked in the lobby when it was slow.

Over time, Sam got sicker and sicker. He started going to the hospital frequently. At some point, he went to the hospital and they kept him there. When I called to ask how he was doing, I learned that the situation wasn't getting any better. I don't remember what, exactly, was wrong with him. It might have been a lot of things. Unfortunately, I also had to tell him when I called that he hadn't paid his rent.

"You're at risk of being evicted, Sam," I said.

His response was, "I don't care."

Weeks later, the coroner called to tell me that Sam had died in the hospital. They said they hadn't been able to successfully locate any of his family members, which made me so sad. Sam, like so many other Cecil tenants, was left unclaimed after his death. Nobody showed up for him. Nobody cared. Maybe nobody knew.

At some point, I remembered that once, Sam had mentioned to me that he had a sister in Colorado. Was that a fact or a fake fact? I wasn't really sure, but I did manage to find a woman who possibly could have been Sam's sister on Facebook. I sent her a message. I never heard back.

To return to my early days at the Cecil, even though the conditions were imperfect, troubleshooting problems with Cindy and Steve was so exciting in the beginning, and I felt incredibly lucky, too. How many people get the opportunity to redesign a hotel in their lifetime? How many people get to work a job that utilizes their creative skills? It was challenging and fun, and I was thrilled to be working with Cindy and Steve, who were such close friends. We all had our own unique roles. Steve was the one in charge. He oversaw everything. Cindy worked on a remote basis. She'd swoop in, offer her opinions, and then head back to Manhattan Beach, and I would stay behind to implement the changes. From the moment I arrived at the Cecil, I was there nonstop, and I was just so glad to be there. The fact that Cindy and I had such unequal roles didn't bother me at first, and I didn't even mind it when Steve paid me late, which happened regularly. As I had at all my other jobs, I naturally took on a massive amount of responsibility with genuine enthusiasm.

There are so many things to consider when you're designing a hotel room. What is the style? What is the color scheme? Window treatments? Bedding? Carpet?

Cindy and I had a blast making all of these choices together, although by "together," I mean that she had final say. Still, it was fine. We had mostly the same tastes anyway. Cindy decided that Stay's main colors should be orange and blue. She's also the one who came up with the name Stay. We agreed that the vibe should be modern, vibrant, and youthful. Along with redesigning the rooms, we also created a community room, complete with a foosball table, a TV, and computers so that our guests could use the internet.

After making the design decisions with Cindy, I did the day-to-day labor. Cindy and I would choose paint colors and items from so many different vendors, including IKEA, and then Pedro and I would drive around town in the Clunker (which is what we called his old minivan) to get them ourselves. IKEA and Home Depot became our homes away from home. And the time in the Clunker allowed Pedro and me to solidify our bond. One day after a trip to Home Depot, he introduced me to pupusas (I'd had no idea what those were). He also took me to a fruit truck, where I ate mango with chili on it for the first time (I hadn't known that was an option) and to a couple of different churro places in neighborhoods I wasn't familiar with at all. Our errands became so much more fun because there were culinary adventures attached to them, and because Pedro and I just had a good time together.

We also had the same work ethic, which was paramount to our copacetic relationship at the hotel. I appreciated that Pedro was task-oriented and fast like me. And, like me, he had a sense of humor. When Steve would call him Pablo by accident, he would just laugh. Pedro not only brought lightness to any situation, he was also the key to getting anything done. He literally had about five hundred keys strapped to his belt, so if you ever needed to unlock a door, you had to go through him. And if you ever needed to know something about the Cecil's history, Pedro was the guy to ask.

The process of redesigning the Stay rooms couldn't have been more hands-on. I loved it. I was learning so much about how the hospitality business worked, being exposed to new groups of people, and using my creative skills. I showed up with exuberance every day, ready to go.

Cindy's attitude, meanwhile, shifted over time from friendly to domineering. It seemed as though the power had gone to her head, and she treated me differently as a result. It was disheartening and confusing. Who did she think she was? And where had my sweet pal gone? Sometimes I felt resentful, but there were so many positive things happening at the same time that it was hard to dwell on it.

While many of the Cecil's architectural features made our lives harder, some of them offered pure excitement. What did we want to do with the abandoned minimart? We would turn it into a coffee-house! What about the retail space located directly next to the Stay lobby? Because Cindy and I were both fascinated by art, we decided to turn that into an art gallery. We would call it, simply, Arty, and we would call the coffeehouse Marty. For a while, we also had plans to turn the empty retail space on the other side of the Cecil lobby into a restaurant named Tuck, and a nook in the lobby that housed a vending machine into a bar called Nip. Those plans were on hold, though, because as long as we were labeled as a residential hotel, getting a liquor license was not an option.

Looking back, it's amazing to think about the DIY flavor of the early days. Since it was basically just Steve, Cindy, and me running the show, it felt like anything was possible. We could invent something, and then it could materialize! There was a Wild West vibe in the beginning that I think of very fondly now. It's also sort of surprising to think about how much power I was given, even though I had zero experience in the world of hotels aside from checking into them. I was just figuring things out on the fly. It seemed like everything was coming together perfectly—and then we got a stop work order from the City of LA.

CHAPTER 4

More Responsibility

During my time at the Cecil, there were so many lawsuits that it became standard procedure for me to show up at the courthouse for a case as the hotel representative or listen in on or give a deposition.

2009 / Cup Noodles

In 2009, a tenant was walking down the hall with a Cup Noodles. We'll call her Destiny. Destiny was very pregnant, and I assumed that she might have been actively smoking crack, too, because multiple people had complained about the metallic smell wafting out of her room. On the walk down the hall with her Cup Noodles, Destiny fell.

The paramedics were called. They examined her. One of them asked if the baby she was about to have was her first, and she said, "No, I have nine children." That made me wonder where those children had gone. I'd never heard Destiny mention them.

Months after this incident, Destiny was evicted because she stopped paying her rent. Time passed. And then one day, she walked up to the front desk.

"Hey, Destiny," I said. I was friendly and warm. Despite the eviction, we had a good relationship—or at least that's what I thought.

"Hi, Amy," she said. And then she told me why she'd shown up. Her baby, she claimed, had been injured on the day she fell with the cup of soup, and she wanted to collect some money for that. Apparently, she felt it was the hotel's fault that she'd fallen.

"I'm so sorry," I said. "How injured is your baby? And where is your baby?"

"With family," she said.

"Oh, that's nice. What's the baby's name?"

There was a long pause, and then she said, "Peter."

Her hesitation made her seem very questionable. Who doesn't remember their baby's name? I hoped that she was lying about the baby being injured—that would have been horrible—but if that was true, then I wondered if perhaps her alleged crack use had also played a role.

Destiny's litigious claims never materialized into a lawsuit. She turned out to be much less determined than many of the other tenants. After I said, "I'm sorry, Destiny. I wish I could help you, but I can't," she left.

2013 / Water

In 2013, after Elisa Lam's body was found, guests sued for reduction of services because there was no water. They were granted a settlement.

2016 / Sleeping on the Job

In 2016, shortly after filing a complaint about a security guard, I got served in the lobby. (I got served so many times during my ten years at the Cecil that even now, I'm still scared someone might walk up to me and hand me some papers and say, "You've been served!") The security guard (let's call him Paul) worked for a third-party company. The reason I fired Paul was because it came to my attention that he was sleeping on the job. Actually, both Paul and the night auditor were sleeping on the couch in the middle of the night. This was discovered when somebody reviewed the camera footage. The most shocking part was that Paul had even brought his own blanket.

I called the third-party company and told them what was happening. Paul's boss, in response, ended up firing him. Sleeping on the job was not acceptable. Then—and actually, this is more shocking than the fact that he brought his own blanket—Paul sued me. For defamation of character. And emotional distress. And psychological distress. He requested a $5,000 settlement.

Then this story got more surprising. A show called *The People's Court* contacted me. It's been on the air since 1981, which is a good indication of how much viewers like to watch surprising (and often ridiculous) cases unfold. As I understand it, the way *The People's Court* finds its cases is to go through public records. Every court case is easily accessible online. From the pile of recent cases, the most jaw-dropping (and ridiculous) ones are chosen to potentially put on the air.

Well, I received a letter from *The People's Court* that read: "We are interested in reviewing the case filed against you by Paul Henry for $5,000. Please be advised *The People's Court* was not contacted by your plaintiff, we are just a neutral party." I should probably point out that the hotel wasn't being sued. Paul was suing me personally.

The letter went on:

The benefits are, you'll receive $250 for your time should the judge rule in your favor, you will not have to pay should the judge rule in your favor or the plaintiff. In addition, there is no report made to your personal record. We will arrange for your travel at no cost, we will save you time, only doing 10 cases a day, as opposed to hundreds at the scheduled local court. The court allows you to be in and out of quickly. Once the case is decided in our forum, the matter is closed forever. The plaintiff cannot appeal a decision or take you back on this matter. We do not have to use your company or last name. Please call us to discuss. Thanks for your time.

So basically, for $250 and some airtime on TV, I was being asked to fly to Connecticut to resolve the case. I rejected the offer, called the third-party company that Paul worked for, and told them what was going on. They took my side in court (which I showed up for in LA), and I won the case because he never showed up.

When I say I learned a lot about the law during my time at the Cecil, these claims are what I'm thinking about. I had been unaware of how people took advantage of the legal system for their own benefit, and how popular it was to lie in court. Before I got the job at the Cecil, my only firsthand experience with courtrooms was as a teenager when my parents had gotten divorced. My general belief was that justice prevailed, that the good guys won, and that laws worked.

Recently, I went to the Salvation Army to shop around. While I was there, a man dropped off a bunch of donations, including a cane. The person who worked at the Salvation Army said, "Sorry, we can't take that." And immediately I knew why. If someone got injured using that cane, they'd sue the Salvation Army. This is how I see the world now: as a place where "justice" has nebulous meanings.

The City of LA lawsuit was probably the most important one, because it defined the Cecil's future.

Here's how it began: a tenant named Simon Bailey (you'll be hearing about him in more detail later) went to the housing department and claimed that all the shared bathrooms had been locked. This was completely untrue, but the housing department didn't know that. Ultimately, Simon Bailey has nothing to do with the lawsuit. He just instigated a meeting between the Cecil and the housing department. When they arrived to inspect the case, it was brought to our attention that the Cecil had been designated as a residential hotel and there were different rules to follow.

Like some of the other hotels in the area, the options at the Cecil allowed for homeless and lower-income folks to pay for rooms by the week, by the month, or by the year. The rule is that if a guest stays at a hotel for longer than thirty days, then it becomes technically "residential," which is to say no longer a hotel at all. It's more like an apartment building. What was confusing was that the Cecil was both. Part of it was inhabited by tenants who'd been living there for years. The other part of it was open to guests.

When the owners learned about the residential designation of the hotel (which, as I mentioned earlier, they claimed to have known nothing about prior to the arrival of the housing department), they wanted to phase out the tenants. This would have been the only way for the Cecil to ever meet its potential as a profitable business, because being designated as a residential hotel meant that there were specific restrictions. For example, construction would not be allowed, and therefore the plan to become a Best Western or something like it would be impossible. You can't have a Best Western unless you have en suite bathrooms, and you couldn't have en suite bathrooms at the Cecil without a massive reconstruction of the entire piping system. This is why it is important to say that we always said our renovation to create Stay was a "cosmetic makeover." No hammers required.

Basically, Stay was a Band-Aid. In a press release issued on July 28, 2008, it is described as a concept that's "part inspiration, part necessity." The press release goes on to say that after a team "purchased the 81-year-old property in May 2007 for $26.5 million, they announced plans for a five-year, $7 million renovation that would transform the entire 15-story, 600-room building into an affordable tourist hotel. Those plans were stymied, however, by the Cecil's inclusion on the city Housing Department's official list of residential hotels, which are protected from conversion or demolition."

In this press release, Steve is quoted as saying, "There's only so much we can do in terms of a renovation to the entire hotel, and we wanted to do what we can now."

When the housing department arrived and saw the work that

we were doing for Stay, they issued a stop work order. This had no impact on us in real time. We were barred from doing any construction, but we weren't doing construction anyway. All of the changes we made to create Stay were cosmetic. I remember that using this word was very important after we got the stop work order. "Cosmetic." We were painting rooms and changing light fixtures. It wasn't a big deal.

The future of the hotel, though, was a big deal, and that's why the owners, in reaction to the stop work order, sued the City of LA. They wanted the "residential" designation removed. If that didn't happen, then the building they'd bought would be essentially worthless. A lot was at stake, and we would have to wait two years to find out the verdict.

In the meantime, the show went on. I got used to my commute from Hermosa Beach and to parking next to the sketchy alley. I became accustomed to the grandeur of the Cecil looming over me as I walked through the entrance. I became more familiar with the tenants at the Cecil, and with the way that some of them were suspicious of me and Steve. They wanted to know who we were and why we were making these changes. The tenants who were mentally ill and prone to paranoia were especially suspicious. There was nothing to do but reassure them that the existence of Stay would not threaten their homes at the Cecil.

My first memory of eviction is set in my mind like cement. Her name was Pebbles, which happened to be the name of my first dog growing up, so I never forgot it. Pebbles was possibly in her late sixties, although her hard lifestyle might have made her look older than she was. I have no idea how long she'd lived there, because she'd arrived long before I had, but my guess is that it was many years. As with all evictions, this one began when Pebbles stopped paying her rent. Before I tell you the details of Pebbles's story, let me first explain the protocol for evictions.

In 2008, this was all brand-new to me. I actually don't even remember how I learned about this process, or how it became my responsibility to evict people. Keep in mind that I'd been hired to redesign one room, and less than a year later, I was evicting tenants. How did that happen? It happened because I was there and I was willing to step in. It didn't necessarily feel like a choice; it just felt like the only reasonable thing to do. Nobody else was raising their hand and saying, *I'll take on evictions!* This was how my job description kept growing and growing. I was always the one who volunteered.

Now, on to the protocol: The first step was to notify the tenant that they needed to pay their rent, and that if they failed to do so, they'd be served an eviction notice. If the tenant didn't respond to the notification, then the next step was to evict them. The physical process of eviction was handled by the sheriff's department. A law enforcement official would come and knock on the door and say, *You need to leave.* Normally, tenants were gone by the time the sheriffs arrived. The sheriffs would knock, no one would answer, and then Pedro would open the door to verify that the room was empty, which it almost always was. After that point, the room would be legally returned to our inventory. The tenant no longer had ownership rights. Any personal property that had been left in the room was bagged up and thrown away.

Back to Pebbles: she had not responded to her eviction notice, but when the sheriffs arrived and knocked on the door, she answered.

"Hey, you want to come in?"

The lighthearted tone of her voice made it clear that she might not have understood the terrible thing that was about to happen to her.

Then she opened the door, at which point the sheriffs, Pedro, and I entered her room. She seemed unworried to see us all there, and then she said, "I'm a medical doctor."

None of us were sure what to make of this.

"I'm a medical doctor," she repeated, and then she repeated it again and again and again.

I remember looking at her and thinking, *I would be surprised to find out that you're really a medical doctor.*

The sheriffs ended up calling the paramedics. What else were they going to do? Handcuff Pebbles and throw her out on the street? When the paramedics arrived, they strapped Pebbles to a stretcher.

"I'm a medical doctor!"

She wouldn't stop saying that. As they rolled her out of the room, I realized she wasn't wearing any shoes.

When someone is mentally ill, they're generally admitted to a facility for seventy-two hours and then they're free to go. This is what happened with Pebbles. After she was released, she returned to the Cecil. Because she hadn't understood that she was being evicted, she still considered the Cecil to be her home. Technically, when a person has been evicted, they're no longer allowed on the property, so when Pebbles came back, we informed her that she couldn't come in.

Pebbles, instead of leaving, stood outside the hotel for three full days. I remember it rained a lot during those days, and still, she didn't move. She stayed right outside the glass doors with her eyes wide open, looking in. And then finally, on the third day, she left.

Before Pebbles, I didn't know anything about how evictions actually worked, and I had never really thought about where mentally ill people go when they have no one to care for them. I guess I'd assumed that we had better systems in place to keep our fellow citizens safe and fed, but we don't. We are lacking in resources, and this is especially true in downtown LA, where 911 is a really popular number.

What happens to the people who exist on the fringes of society? Where do people like Pebbles go after they've been kicked to the curb? And how was it fair to expect someone who was confused about her own identity to not be confused about the fact that she needed to pay rent? While it might not have been fair, what else were we supposed to do?

Seeing Pebbles stand outside in the rain was the first time I felt completely powerless. I am a helper. It's in my nature to want to be supportive, even to people I don't know. Watching Pebbles, it became clear to me that I wasn't going to be able to help everyone at the Cecil who was suffering. There were about eighty tenants when I arrived. It wasn't possible to know that many people closely.

This was a question I would get used to asking during my time at the Cecil: "What else are we supposed to do?" How responsible is a residential hotel for the fates of its tenants? After Pebbles left, I certainly never received a call informing me that she'd found a suitable place to live. She, like so many others, just disappeared.

During this period, Pedro and I hung out for the first time outside of work. His daughter called to invite me to his fiftieth birthday party. I was the first one to arrive. Pedro was outside boiling oil for carnitas, and when he saw me, he was surprised. His daughter hadn't told him that I was coming. I know he was happy, too. We'd become real friends by then.

Since Pedro was the hotel's unofficial historian, he told me more about its sordid past as time went on. Once, he said, somebody had jumped off the ninth floor and survived. Often, he told me, when somebody died, the money would be stolen from their pockets. All of this was shocking, but Pedro's wry sense of humor continued to make it seem somehow bearable. Another thing he told me was that whenever somebody passed away, he looked at the dead body. I think it was purely out of curiosity. Many years into my time at the Cecil, though, he would stop looking. Dead bodies freaked me out, so I avoided them, almost completely. I did see plenty of them coming and going, but they were already in body bags, being rolled out. I saw only one the entire time I was at the hotel, and it still haunts me.

Honestly, it was horribly difficult to avoid dead bodies at the Cecil.

One day, I was sitting in my office when I heard the thunderous landing of an object hitting the sub-roof just above me. I ran to the front desk immediately and asked the agents on duty, "What was that noise?"

Neither agent knew what I was talking about. The sound had been too far away from them to hear.

Then the phone rang. I picked it up. "Front desk," I said.

The caller was DJ and he was hysterical. "A man just jumped from the building and landed right in front of my room. He's dead."

For some reason, that's exactly what I had thought it was going to be. That thunderous sound—it just sounded like a body.

I called 911 and told them about the man.

"Is there any sign of breathing?" the operator asked.

I said the same thing I'd said after Elisa Lam's body was found. "I think you better just head over."

While we waited for the police, we found the room that the man had jumped from. It was on the ninth floor. As I mentioned earlier, the Cecil was still on the key system, not the key-card system. And, when keys were lost there was always a risk of someone trying to come back and access guest rooms—just by going door to door. The key system is old fashioned and not foolproof. We didn't have the money to upgrade these locks. We could barely keep the lights on. This meant that if the key to a room got into the wrong hands, the person who received it could walk freely into the hotel, go up to the room, and squat. It would have been easy to squat for a while because after a tenant left, their room remained empty.

This was the case with the room the man had jumped from. There wasn't even a bed inside, and the man, it turned out, was not staying with us. He had trespassed. Maybe someone had given him a key, or he'd broken in somehow. He'd jumped from a room that was out of order, which means there wasn't any furniture inside.

When the police arrived, I escorted the officers to the empty room on the ninth floor. I hadn't been in the room before that moment. Plugged into the wall was a cell phone, charging. A plastic bag filled with clothes said PATIENT BELONGINGS on it. One officer started going through the bag. The other was looking out the window. The windows at the Cecil were very old, single-panel sliders with flimsy screens. Most hotels have windows you can't open so far. So many of our rooms were out of order that we didn't have those in place.

"How bad does it look?" I asked the officer standing by the window. I have no idea why. What was I expecting him to say?

"It's not bad at all," the officer responded. "It looks like it's right out of the movies. There's barely any blood at all. You should come and take a look."

I remember standing there, staring at the officer and considering my options. Why was I considering looking at a dead body at all? Was it because I knew that my time at the Cecil was almost up? Was it because the police officer was encouraging me to come and take a look?

As I walked to the window, I felt like my heart was going to explode out of my chest. Once I got there, I waited a moment. I became aware of the familiar flimsy screen that was now open from the edge of the window, and I tuned in to how high up we were. I had never experienced a fear of heights before working at the Cecil, but I definitely left with one. I wonder how much this particular incident had to do with that.

Finally, I looked down.

And saw a perfectly chiseled male body. He was young, in his twenties, sprawled on the sub-roof in a pair of white underpants with his eyes wide open. Even from the ninth floor, I could see the whites of his eyes and a small line of blood trickling from his head across the cement. I couldn't believe how beautiful he was, and how white his skin was. Unlike many of the other people who frequented the Cecil, his body bore no signs of a hard life.

Why had this young man ended his life? Did he have family? Parents? Kids?

These were some of the questions that flooded my mind.

At some point, one of the officers checked the phone that was charging and said, "It's been wiped clean." Did that mean that the death was premeditated? Why would someone remove all the data from their phone and then charge it?

As I stood there looking at the body, it dawned on me that the man's face looked kind of familiar. I finally realized that yes, he'd been a guest at Stay on Main—which had formally been called Stay; more on this soon—several weeks earlier. We'd been forced to ask him to leave because he didn't have the money to pay for his room. This was a very common problem at the property, so it wasn't that memorable.

But then the man did become more memorable.

About a week after he was asked to leave, he was found walking the hallways of the second floor naked, during breakfast time, while the Stay on Main guests were trying to enjoy their complimentary cereal and coffee.

The front desk agent recorded the incident:

At around 9:10am, a man came into the hotel. He looked suspicious and was talking to himself. He started to walk up the stairs. By the time security arrived a few minutes later, the man was making a big scene and was naked, so he was asked to leave. He was going crazy and either hitting or throwing something, which I couldn't see but it was loud and scary. We did end up calling the police. They took the guy.

After this note was received, the man was put on the blacklist.

A while after his death, I went to a spin class during my lunch break, which I almost never did. Usually, I exercised after work, but on that day, I felt out of sorts, and I thought some cycling would help. After the class, I entered the locker room and checked my phone. I saw that I had a missed call from the Cecil.

When I called back, the agent at the front desk informed me that the man's father was at the hotel and wanted to speak to me.

My initial thought was, *Oh, he's going to try to sue us*. Given history, this seemed very plausible.

I drove back to the hotel and entered my office from the back door. Then I called down to the front desk and asked where the man's father was. The agent told me that he was outside, in front of the hotel, waiting for me.

I felt like my legs went numb as I walked through the lobby. I was so uneasy. Would I have felt that way if I hadn't seen the body? I think I probably would have, but seeing the body made it even harder.

The man's father was in his fifties, wearing clean clothes. He seemed well-meaning. He told me that he was a retired New York Police officer, and that he and his wife had a preplanned trip prior to his son's death to visit their kids in California.

His wife, he told me, was nearby in their rental car, too afraid and upset to get out.

This answered my question about the man's family.

"Have you ever lost anyone you loved?" the father asked me.

That question, which he asked very seriously, hit me hard. I think it changed the entire dynamic of our meeting, too. I had started out wanting to maintain a professional distance, but after he said that, it became personal.

Had I ever lost anyone I loved?

Of course, I thought of the moment I'd learned my dad had unexpectedly died of a stomach aneurysm several years before. So I told him that. "My father," I said.

He nodded in understanding. A few moments passed. And then he told me why he had come to the hotel. "I want to see where my son died," he said.

Instinctively, I tried to ascertain whether or not this could potentially have negative consequences for us later. If he saw something awry, was he going to take us to court?

Weirdly (or not weirdly; he was a cop), the father read my mind. "I'm not here to sue you," he said. "I just want you to show me where he died."

After a pause, I said, "I believe you. I'll show you."

Maybe it was because he was a police officer that the father was able to keep his composure as we made our way up to the ninth floor. He seemed incredibly stable. I, meanwhile, felt unhinged. In the elevator, I said, "I saw your son. He was so beautiful. And it looked like he had so much potential. If you don't mind me asking, what happened?"

The father thought for a moment, and then he told me that his son, back in high school, had been the captain of the football team. "He had a real life ahead of him," the father said, "and then it went off the rails."

He told me that for the last several years, his son had struggled with mental illness. He didn't give a specific diagnosis, but he did say that on the day he'd jumped, his son had checked out of the mental ward of a hospital. So this explained the bag that said PATIENT BELONGINGS on it.

"I spoke to him on the phone that day," the father said. "I thought he sounded good."

Then the story got even sadder. The son had a son himself back on the East Coast, the father told me.

We walked down the hallway of the ninth floor together. I unlocked the door to the room his son had jumped from. He went inside and looked out the window. After that I offered to take him to where they had found his son's body.

Once we got down there, I stepped away and was quiet. I wanted to give him some space. The father stood there, staring at the cement for a few minutes. I stood off to the side, hoping he felt a healing sense of closure.

Shortly after this experience, the young man who had died popped up on my Facebook page as someone I might know. It was so chilling to see.

Despite the horrendous things happening around us, we had to keep going. For the few months after we got the stop work order, we continued making cosmetic changes to what would soon become Stay. We had all the doors with the dents in them buffed out and the extra locks removed. Then we installed new locks that would accommodate a key-card system, which was easier and would allow us to have an electronic record of guests coming and going from their rooms. We put the finishing touches on the community room and the new lobby. Next to the front desk, Steve placed a large fiberglass dog statue, which sort of became Stay's mascot (and which he would steal later on, after his relationship with the owners went south).

After we installed the new furnishings for the rooms, we had a big furniture sale with all the old stuff, a lot of which had been purchased in the '70s. This included dressers and ancient TV sets that had to be separated with tools, because at the Cecil, TV sets were bolted down to the dressers so that people couldn't steal them. Everything sold very quickly, including our aged and soiled mattresses, which went to a mattress refurbisher. Every time I see an old pickup truck loaded with dirty mattresses I think of the Cecil. Apparently, there's an entire business centered around stripping old mattresses and reselling them. This is one of the many facts about the world that I might never have learned had I not worked at the Cecil.

Generally, I'm not sure that an interior designer would take charge of a furniture sale, but that was the spirit of the job, which seemed to match my constitution perfectly. I took on projects that had nothing to do with my original job description, and what this led to was more responsibility. After finishing the interior redesign of Stay, I didn't leave. Instead, I assumed a new title: brand manager.

CHAPTER 5

I Hope This Works

The closer we got to opening Stay, the more there was to do, and my title of brand manager didn't accurately explain all the new responsibilities I took on. In many ways, it was like I'd slipped into managing the hotel already. Some people had begun to refer to me as the Mayor, which was flattering. In truth, though, titles weren't important to me. All I cared about was that the hotel survived.

There are so many elements that need to be in place before a hotel can start operating. How much were we going to charge? What amenities would we offer? How would we advertise? What about listing on sites like Expedia? Who was going to run the front desk? What about the employee handbook?

I didn't know the answers to a lot of these questions at first. Actually, I wasn't even aware of what the correct questions were. An employee handbook? I probably never would have thought of that on my own. But when Steve brought to my attention that we needed one,

I figured it out. As with all the other problems that arose, I learned to solve them by solving them.

When I arrived in 2007, the Cecil barely had an online presence. That made sense, because well over 50 percent of its business was from people walking in off the street and paying in cash. I remember there was one negative review about the Cecil online that said something to the effect of, *This is where people go to die.*

Clearly, if we wanted to be successful at all, we would need to commit to branding ourselves as a completely separate property. But it was hard to escape the old property. I mean this both figuratively (would it be possible to leave our old reputation behind?) and geographically: the only thing that separated the Cecil lobby and the Stay lobby was our coffeehouse, Marty. The best we could do, in terms of rebranding ourselves, was to make a bunch of changes. So that's exactly what we did.

Because Stay was marketed toward the modern traveler who was willing to pay a little more, we charged $65 for a room with only a sink and $85 for a room that included a shower and a toilet. (The Cecil charged $45 and $65.) We also offered a cheaper option for guests on a smaller budget: rooms with bunk beds that offered enough space for up to six people.

Another difference was the method of payment. Unlike at the Cecil, where people mostly paid cash, we required that all guests give us a credit card number in order to hold a room. We also required that they give us their IDs when they checked in. (Later, this rule would also be implemented at the Cecil.) All of these choices led to progress. Higher rates meant more money. And getting more strict on policies would deter criminals from checking in, or at least that was the hope.

In addition to these obvious benefits, there were the unforeseen ones. At night, from the hours of about eleven p.m. to seven a.m., the only person in the hotel lobby was the night auditor. The main duty of the night auditor was to check in the guests who arrived late and reconcile the previous day's financial reports. But most of the time, there wasn't much for them to do. This gave the night auditors a lot of time to identify loopholes and take advantage of them. Since the Cecil was on a traditional key system, which was untraceable, and since most people paid in cash, it was a little bit too easy for the night auditor to give a guest a key and pocket the cash. At Stay, breaking the rules in this way would be much less likely.

In order to avoid hiring extra employees, we decided that the people who worked the front desk at the Cecil would also work the front desk at Stay—but in different uniforms. This meant that sometimes, an employee would cross over from one lobby to the other and have to change their shirt. Of course, there were many differences between these two lobbies. Stay had a sculpture of a dog in it just for fun, whereas the Cecil lobby was nowhere close to the idea of "fun." The most noticeable difference, especially in the summer, was that the Stay lobby was air-conditioned. This was an exciting perk of its history as a lens shop. On hot days, guests could walk into the Stay lobby and breathe a sigh of relief. And then—well, and then they'd leave the lobby and head toward the elevators, and this was where the populations of the Cecil and Stay would meet.

Was this going to be a problem, or was it going to be okay?

Before Stay opened, we got to pretend like it wasn't going to be that big of a problem. We got to live in the amazing potential of our little hostel, which seemed like it could save the entire property—well, until we learned of the result of the lawsuit.

In the meantime, I set up meetings with companies like Expedia and Booking.com in the hopes of reaching as many customers as possible. Cindy, who was a writer, composed all the necessary copy. I took photos of the rooms. I also set up a Yelp page and met with Cisco to decide on what would be included in our complimentary breakfast.

Every decision seemed to turn into five decisions, and the breakfast is a good example. Did we want waffles? Bananas? Eggs? Eggs were way too expensive, so we passed on those. For a while, we tried bananas, but those ended up being too expensive as well. In the end, we kept it as bare-bones as possible: cereal, coffee, tea. The idea was the less that could be potentially stolen by non-guests wandering into the breakfast room, the better.

Steve, at some point, schooled me on bedbugs. He said when there are bedbugs there will always be blood on the sheets, that that was clear evidence of an infestation. I remember him telling me that, and me relaying it to the housekeeping staff through Pedro, who translated in Spanish. Later, I would learn that bedbugs, like old soiled mattresses, are the centerpiece of an entire industry—run by con artists. As it turns out, it's not uncommon for people to bring their own bedbugs to a hotel, set them free on the bed, and then claim that the hotel has bedbugs in order to get their stay for free.

Where do you get live bedbugs?

eBay, apparently.

A few years after the opening of Stay, we would get sued by a lawyer whose billboard advertisements were framed as questions: GOT BEDBUGS? CALL ME! One of our guests called the 1–800 number after allegedly having found some bedbugs in their room. This was one of the many, many lawsuits I handled on behalf of the hotel. I can't remember if we won this case or not, but I do know that bedbugs are an issue for every hotel and that they're an expensive and arduous problem to fix.

The other thing I did before we opened was make friends with our neighbors. I made flyers with discount codes and walked around downtown handing them out. "If you have friends coming into town, tell them to use this discount code!" I formed a lot of collaborative partnerships in this way. I would send guests to nearby businesses, and the businesses would send patrons to us. It was so exciting to describe the new, cool modern hostel that was about to be born, and it was equally exciting that our neighbors had savvy ventures of their own. We were forming a new community, one that would rejuvenate the streets of downtown LA—or at least that's how it felt at the time.

Another form of community outreach, if you could call it that, was when Pedro and I took the fiberglass dog all over the city and took pictures of it in front of landmarks. You have to have fun making your marketing materials, right? Well, we not only had a lot of fun. We also got into trouble. At Griffith Park, a ranger informed us that taking photos of the park for commercial use was prohibited. Thankfully, we'd gotten all the pictures we needed by the time that happened.

Along with all the preparations any hotel would have to make, we had the extra job of transforming our abandoned retail spaces. We successfully converted the old minimart into Marty, the cute coffeehouse where guests could hang out. We also put a call out on Craigslist for artists to submit their work to be considered for our first gallery show at Arty. A large number of people responded, and it was up to Cindy and me to choose who would be the best fit. Dipping into the world of artists and art-making was extremely fulfilling for me at the time, although now, I can also see that it was a way to avoid marketing my own art. I was operating as a shadow artist, investing my time in the creations of others but still too afraid to show my own. A more positive way to consider Arty would be to say that it was a step in the right direction. I was inserting myself into a world that interested me, and proximity to working artists was inspirational.

The feeling in the air was one of hope—but there were many variables that were working against us. In addition to the ones I've mentioned so far (the shared elevators, the proximity to Skid Row, the Cecil's haunted history, the fact that Stay only consisted of 138 out of 600 rooms), there were also the coroner vans that were frequently parked outside the entrance.

Here's another note from the front desk.

At about 3pm room 831 had not checked out. I sent security to open her door, which was deadbolted. I had a feeling something was wrong. She displayed erratic behavior when I helped her yesterday. The documentation we have for her also states she is mentally ill. Security called me via radio and I went up to the floor to assess the situation. The room was a complete mess. Lamp was broken, food everywhere. There were also empty alcohol and prescription containers. She was snoring and breathing but her face and lips were purple. I decided to call paramedics because she did not look well. Paramedics came and took her. LAPD later called me and told me that she pulled through and that we could proceed with cleaning the room.

I'd become accustomed to asking the coroner vans to drive around to the back alley so that our new guests wouldn't see the evidence of death. Some of the drivers moved without complaint, and

CHAPTER 6

The Early Days of Stay

In the fall of 2008, Stay was officially born, and I was feeling a confusing mix of hope and anxiety. I suppose that all the years before the lawsuit ended can be categorized by this dichotomy. On the one hand, we were making progress! According to the July 2008 press release, "Industry observers predict that Stay could find success in Downtown Los Angeles!" On the other hand, would we ever make true progress?

Alongside the travelers pulling up at the curb with their suitcases when we first opened, there were protesters with signs who claimed that our presence was negatively affecting the longtime tenants of the Cecil. Along with the coroner vans showing up to collect dead bodies, there were our hilarious marketing schemes to get people interested in the hotel.

The first was called Stay in a Bubble, which a press release dated October 2008 describes perfectly:

"In celebration of its arrival, Stay will display live hotel guests living 24 hours per day in two model rooms that we have created in street-level storefront windows, fully visible from Main Street. Initially, these guests—Ashley, Alicia, Toby, Zac, and Casey—will be on display until November 15, 2008, although the promotion may be extended for an indefinite period of time."

The bubble dwellers in question were all models and hopeful actors and actresses, which we hoped would give Stay a certain allure. I contacted Apple to get them free iPods and laptops (which were surprisingly easy to get), and Red Bull to provide complimentary beverages. For a time, we thought this idea was brilliant. It got people talking. Passersby would look in on the good-looking people who had agreed to live behind a glass storefront. And then, unfortunately, some of the models turned out to be very difficult. Eventually, they left. I assumed we wouldn't attempt the same shtick again, but then an agent representing a gothic rock band from Germany contacted me asking if they could live in the bubble. I was wary at first, but I said yes anyway, and I'm so glad that I did, because the band members turned out to be lovely people who became my friends. I actually attended one of their weddings in Germany a few years ago. It's amazing to me that a band that wore full makeup and partied all hours of the night could cause fewer problems than the hired actors. Prior to my interaction with the band, I would have stereotyped them as a major potential problem.

On top of the exciting press that we drummed up for ourselves, there were the magazines and news outlets that gave us glowing reviews. In 2009, Delta's *Sky* magazine named us one of the top ten budget hotels in the country. Here's their description:

"Mod hotel-hostel hybrid with private rooms as well as rooms with shared quarters and/or facilities, each packed with playful details. Coming soon: restaurant Tuck and the bar Nip. Private rooms start at $85."

Around the same time, *Budget Travel* magazine devoted an entire page to us, complete with a picture of our fiberglass dog and flowered wallpaper. A section called "The 'Hood" reads:

"Once-sketchy Main Street is currently on the upswing (Johnny Depp and Katherine Heigl both have lofts nearby), but the area can be a little desolate at night."

Another section, called "Unexpected Extras," tells readers about how we handed out Xbox consoles for guests to use in the community room and that Tuck, our comfort food restaurant slated to open the following year, "will deliver meat loaf and milkshakes to your room." This write-up speaks to how popular we were in the beginning. "Although they tend to book weeks in advance, try to nab one of the 13 private rooms that come with [queen-sized pillow-top beds], Eames-style reading lamps and [their own bathrooms]."

The reviews from guests were overwhelmingly positive, too. Young travelers on a budget from all over the world started checking in, just as we'd envisioned. They enjoyed our amenities and our colorful, quirky décor. It was a euphoric time, and a busy one. Something was always happening. We needed more coffee for the café! We needed new artists for the gallery! The guests needed this; the employees needed that. I remember thinking that what I needed was a pair of roller skates so that I could get from one problem to the next faster.

On a typical morning, I'd put on my nice clothes and drive from Hermosa Beach to the Cecil. For a while, I was picking up Steve in Manhattan Beach and bringing him to work with me, because his

Maserati had broken down and he couldn't afford to fix it. Looking back, this probably wasn't a great sign. Who owns a luxury car that they can't afford to repair?

In the spirit of change, Steve terminated a bunch of employees, which meant that we moved out of the conference room and into their offices. Steve took the general manager's office, which was as grand and opulent and anachronistic as the lobby. I should probably mention that for the first few years I worked at the hotel, there were several different general managers, all of whom got fired for one reason or another. Maybe this was why Steve took the office for himself.

I moved into a smaller office near Steve's, but I was so busy that I was barely ever in there. One of my fondest memories of that office is when I taught Pedro how to use the computer. One evening, I remember asking him, in a joking way, if he knew how to turn the computer on. He said yes, and I said, "Prove it." And that's when he revealed that no, he didn't know how to use a computer. So I taught him. It was the least I could do to repay him for introducing me to pupusas.

During the days, the only time I stopped moving was when Pedro and I would take our three p.m. coffee break. Every afternoon, without fail, we'd meet at Marty, do a little catch-up, and then part ways. Even now, when we get together for lunch, we have a coffee together. It's a tradition that's stuck. The best part about Marty, besides meeting Pedro there, was the unlimited free Diet Coke from the soda fountain. I drank it all day every day like a fiend.

Marty was a hit with guests, and so was Arty. I felt especially proud to be running an art gallery, and knew that the only reason I was able to do that was because the Cecil happened to own the space. It's not like we were bringing in a lot of money, but we did get a ton of exposure. During Art Walk, which is an event that showcases the galleries in downtown LA, the place would be filled to the gills with potential clients and people ambling around downtown. My favorite part about Arty was that I got to meet some wonderful artists who would remain friends for years. On paper, Cindy and I were both in charge of Arty, but in reality, our responsibilities were divided in the same way they had been across the board for the previous year: Cindy offered her opinions, and I did everything else.

After work and on the weekends, I continued making my jewelry and selling it. I felt proud of that, and proud of how, in only a little over a year, I had completely switched professions. Somehow, I was running a hotel, an art gallery, and a coffee shop, and I was giving advice to guests about downtown LA, a neighborhood that I'd never expected to know well.

One of my favorite things to recommend was the StarLine, a bus that took tourists on a tour of celebrities' houses. I'd say something like, "You don't need to stay in Hollywood to see Hollywood!" I knew this was why many of our guests had come to LA in the first place. They wanted to see mansions in Beverly Hills and the stars on Hollywood Boulevard, not Skid Row.

The early success of Stay far exceeded our expectations. Steve, Cindy, and I really felt like we were saving the property from financial ruin and helping to uplift the neighborhood at the same time. A more conservative boss might have waited to see how things were going to pan out at our Main Street location before even considering the idea of expansion, but Steve, the guy who bought a Maserati he couldn't afford to fix, was the opposite of conservative. He wanted more, and he wanted it fast. Even before all the rooms at Stay were open to guests, he was talking about opening other locations in San Diego, San Francisco, Hawaii, and Seattle, and then he was flying to those cities to look at properties.

I accompanied Steve on a trip to Seattle to tour a construction site that he thought might be a good Stay location in the future. We spent the day walking around in hard hats and nodding our heads. Later, I went to Honolulu a few times with Steve to do the same thing. Every time we left, I would spend the whole time worrying about how our team in downtown LA was doing without us, but this didn't seem to be on Steve's mind at all. He cared more about opening new locations than he did about the original one. But maybe he was right to have his eye on the future. We were doing so well that an expansion did seem plausible, and I was well aware that if it happened, it might translate to a more all-encompassing job for me. I wouldn't just be the brand manager at one location; I'd be overseeing the brand of a corporation.

At the time, I didn't think Steve's actions were questionable. I trusted him. I thought he was a good guy who'd gotten a little carried away with our cool new concept. It really was intoxicating how much the press and our guests loved us at the beginning. Stay was affordable, modern, and well decorated. People barely seemed to mind the shared elevator bank, or the smells of some of the Cecil tenants. For the first six months, we were riding high on our own success.

And then summer arrived, and so did our first negative reviews.

CHAPTER 7

Problems

The heat made it truly unbearable to be anywhere inside the building that wasn't air-conditioned. Plus, summer is notoriously a busy time for hotels, so it was more crowded than usual, which made it seem even hotter. The fact that we couldn't provide guests with humane temperatures was appalling, and it contradicted our appeal. How could we call ourselves a cutting-edge hostel when we didn't have the basic amenity of central air and had absolutely zero plans to install it?

There were complaints about the heat, of course, but it didn't stop there. If one part of the experience at a hotel is displeasing, then a guest is much more likely to find all the other displeasing elements and name them. As I mentioned earlier, the heat intensified the foul smells of the Cecil and its tenants, and it wasn't hard for our guests to pick up on that, especially within the confined space of the elevator bank. Suddenly, the temporary solution to mix the populations of Stay and of the Cecil stopped working so well. Because of the summertime crowds, guests often had to wait in line to ride the elevator, and during the five to ten minutes they stood there, becoming increasingly annoyed that they couldn't quickly get up to their rooms, it was only natural that they used that time to look a little more closely at the strange characters waiting with them. Also, the elevator bank at Stay overlooked the lobby of the Cecil, so guests had even more of an opportunity to clock the strange behavior of tenants.

If a complaint came to the front desk, the protocol was to immediately comp the room. In the long term, it's much cheaper to do this than it is to weather the impact of a negative online review. Whether it was a complaint about the heat, the long elevator lines, or the strange behavior of the Cecil tenants, the standard response was to apologize for the inconvenience and offer a free stay.

Another note from the front desk:

On the night of 12/19 I had my interaction with Larry in room 1032. I think it was around 1am when a couple checked in next door to room 1031. As soon as they got to the room, I got a phone call from 1032, (not knowing the history between himself & our staff) he complained that the people that had checked into the room next to him were being extremely loud & he wanted something done about it. I sent security up to the room to see what was going on, but they came back down to report that there was no noise coming from that area. About 5 minutes later, not even ten minutes after 1031 checked in, they came back to the lobby and claimed that the man from 1032 had just threatened to murder them and that they didn't feel safe staying in the hotel any longer so they canceled the reservation and got a full refund.

> A suspicious person entered the building and started yelling at
> a female guest for no reason. I called 911. Somehow, we managed
> to get this crazy guy out. The police never showed up.

If a complaint went straight to the internet, there was really nothing we could do about it. Reviews on Expedia and the like are impossible to erase, even if they're outright lies. A lot of businesses, in an attempt to mitigate this, offer incentives, and this is exactly what we did. *Free $5 Starbucks gift cards in exchange for a review!* The incentives were successful, but they didn't completely solve the problem. Even if we hadn't had the glaring issues that we did, people's perceptions can't be controlled. What one guest found unbearable might have been fine to another guest. There was no perfect solution. All we could do was our best.

One unforeseen glitch with adding Stay to sites like Expedia, Orbitz, Travelocity, and Booking.com was we that we had such limited inventory. This sometimes caused us to oversell rooms, especially the ones with en suite bathrooms. When this happened, a guest would arrive, ready to check in at Stay, and we'd have to inform them that unfortunately, their room had been double-booked. "But it's okay," we'd say. "We have rooms at the Cecil!"

If they reacted positively to that offer, we'd send them to the Cecil lobby. And then we'd wait five minutes. Would they return and ask for their money back? Or would they accept the Cecil room? It was nerve-racking, and also felt somewhat embarrassing.

Our presence on the internet offered both positive and negative consequences. Expedia, along with the rest of the sites, got us tons of extra bookings and positive Yelp reviews increased our popularity immensely. But as the unbearably hot summer continued, the negative reviews took their toll. The three floors that comprised Stay, which had been overflowing with guests in the beginning, slowly emptied out, and by the fall of 2009, our income had dipped severely.

How were we going to survive? Steve decided that the best thing to do would be to sell off the rooms in bundle form to organizations. Could a floor of Stay become student housing, for example? The first organizations Steve wanted to target were colleges and universities in the area. Like Stay itself, this seemed like a good idea, or it seemed like the only idea. Stay had evolved as a Band-Aid, and this was another Band-Aid stuck on top of it.

What the plan to sell rooms in bulk to organizations meant for me was that I had more to do. On top of fielding requests and complaints from guests and running Arty and Marty, I also started giving tours to colleges and universities. I'd walk school housing folks through the halls while peppily saying things like, "Wouldn't this be the perfect place for your students? Look at all these amenities!" And then, before I knew it, I was walking representatives from all sorts of organizations through the halls and giving similar spiels that were tailored to their specific needs.

Each organization had different visions. The rehabs envisioned a layout for recovering addicts, and the sheriff's department envisioned a housing for former prisoners. Then, too, along with these types of investors, there were the high-end hotel groups that envisioned installing a rooftop swimming pool—if the verdict of the lawsuit allowed for that.

During all of these tours, I was selling the dream of what the building could become. Meanwhile, there was the problem of what the building currently was: a place where tenants and hotel guests were consistently overdosing, dying, and/or having outbursts in the lobby. Once, while I was giving a tour to a group of potential investors, a man, dressed all in black, with a rifle strapped across his chest, ran down the hall and yelled at me, "Ma'am, get back in your room!" I realized he was a sniper.

When I asked why, the sniper told me that there had been a stabbing and that the perpetrator was on the loose. How could I explain that to the potential investors? Well, I couldn't. Suffice to say, those investors were not interested. Many of the other groups felt the same way. Even though they hadn't been exposed to a sniper trying to catch a criminal in our halls, it was clear for many other reasons that we would not be an uncomplicated investment.

So many people at the Cecil lived alone and were clearly not doing that well, and I remember feeling especially sad for a man named Mr. McCormick, who was not only alone, but also used a wheelchair. His legs ended at his knees, which were wrapped in a combination of ACE bandages and socks. He always seemed to be leaning forward, slumped over himself. It seemed like a posture of defeat. But then, every time he saw me, he perked up and said, "You're so beautiful!"

"Wow," I would say, "thanks."

I felt flattered rather than creeped out by his compliments, and I was glad that flirting with me seemed to make him happy. He was in his seventies, and harmless, and every time I saw him, he was bright and friendly.

At some point, Pedro told me that before Mr. McCormick had lost his legs, he'd frequently bring hookers up to his room. ("Hookers" was the term Pedro used.) It was so hard for me to imagine this sweet old man doing that, but I knew Pedro was telling the truth, because it's not in his nature to lie. When I asked him how Mr. McCormick had lost his legs, Pedro said, "He did it to himself."

"What do you mean he did it to himself?" I asked.

"He lost his legs because he loves sugar too much."

Pedro went on to explain that Mr. McCormick had diabetes and, despite that, had continued to eat massive amounts of sugar. According to Pedro, he was addicted. That made no sense to me. How could you compromise your legs for sugar? It seemed so illogical.

I got used to receiving Mr. McCormick's flirtatious compliments. Every time, I would smile and thank him. Honestly, he brightened my days.

And then, one afternoon, a housekeeper went in for a scheduled cleaning and found him in his wheelchair, slumped over and definitely not breathing. After his body had been removed, I went up with Pedro to evaluate the condition of his room. This was probably the first time I really began to understand how many of our tenants were living with almost nothing. Mr. McCormick owned a few outfits and nothing more. On his night table were several Mountain Dew cans and some candy wrappers, which seemed so incredibly depressing to me. I imagined him sitting alone eating these sugary treats. Did he enjoy them? Did he feel lonely? In the center of the room was his wheelchair. It sat there like a ghost.

After I took in all these details, I noticed Mr. McCormick's collection of journals. There were many of them, and again, I imagined him alone in the room, writing down his thoughts. What *were* his thoughts? Curious, I started reading.

On page after page, Mr. McCormick had written the exact same words. I can't remember exactly what the words were, but I do remember thinking that they were similar to what Jack Nicholson's character writes over and over again in *The Shining*: "All work and no play makes Jack a dull boy." It wasn't until I found his nonsensical journal entries that I realized Mr. McCormick was not mentally stable. We'd had such brief interactions that it had never even crossed my mind to wonder about his mental wellness. This was when I began to catch on to the fact that the appearances of the tenants at the Cecil could not necessarily be trusted.

Our tenants were not only frequently lonely, they were also frequently surprising.

There was a woman named Anne, for example, who Pedro told me had moved to the Cecil long before I'd arrived, with her sister, Brianne. Many times, I asked Pedro if he was sure about this information. "Anne and Brianne? Why would they have such similar names?"

"They're twins," he would say, as if that was an explanation.

I never met Brianne, because she died before I arrived.

When I think of Anne now, what I remember most vividly is her hair. I always gave her compliments about how voluminous it looked. Along with her gorgeous hair, Anne also had a gorgeous face. She was in her midthirties, probably, same as me at the time. I didn't get the sense that she was into drinking or drugs. She seemed more into walking at a very fast pace while having conversations with herself.

What I found interesting about Anne and her conversations was that she'd always snap out of them when she saw me. She'd be completely immersed in whatever she was saying (sometimes it was pornographic), and then, as she walked, she'd look up and say, "Hi, Amy!"

"Hi, Anne, how are you?" I would say.

And then she'd be back in her own conversation, beelining away from me.

There were rumors that Anne would lock herself in the public bathrooms on the tenant floors and masturbate. I never found out if those rumors were true, but her pornographic mutterings made me think they could have been.

Some of the tenants at the Cecil had proper jobs. Anne, meanwhile, was an entrepreneur. She made money by running errands for other tenants. She took her job very seriously, and she was good at it, because she was both diligent and speedy.

One day, Anne asked to see me at the front desk.

"I'm moving out," she said to me.

"Are you sure?" I asked. Moving out of the Cecil was almost unheard of. Where else were tenants like Anne going to go? A lot of them didn't have many other options.

"Yes," Anne said, "I'm positive."

She went on to tell me that she planned to take a bus to Louisiana, which was where her family lived. "I'm ready for a change," she said.

I probably asked her, "Are you sure?" five hundred times. "If you leave, Anne, you can't come back. We're not taking new tenants. Your room will be gone forever." Sometimes you had to explain things in a very simple but clear way. There was always room for miscommunication.

Anne told me she understood. And then she left. I thought I would never see her again.

A few weeks later, a priest from a church in Louisiana called. Apparently, when Anne arrived to her hometown with plans to reunite with her family, she found that their house had been destroyed by Hurricane Katrina. She hadn't been in touch with her family in years and literally hopped on that bus thinking things would be as they were when she had left. The church had raised money to pay for Anne's bus ticket back to Los Angeles, but we couldn't take her back. I do know that she returned, though; I see her all the time. Just recently, Pedro and I were walking around downtown after lunch and there was Anne, scurrying down the street, probably running an errand for somebody.

Another tenant who ended up surprising me was Mr. Sanchez. He was a skinny man in his late seventies who worked as a security guard. Pedro and I used to drive over to Stumptown in the Arts District for our three o'clock break, which is a very popular coffee place in Los Angeles. Often, on the way he'd point at a building nearby and say, "That's where Mr. Sanchez works."

Whenever I saw Mr. Sanchez, I thought, *This man looks so professional.* His clothes were always pressed. He just looked so together. And he was friendly, too. He'd come up to the front desk and chat gregariously. Sometimes he'd praise my clothes. "Oh, Amy, I love your outfit!" he'd exclaim.

Once in a while, he'd mention his girlfriend, who was apparently my age and had a similar sense of style. "Sara would love this outfit!" I suppose I was surprised to learn that Mr. Sanchez had a girlfriend half his age, and I wondered why I'd never met her. Was she a fantasy? Or was I being judgmental?

One day, Mr. Sanchez was found dead in his room. He'd died of natural causes. When his nephew came by to pick up the belongings, he found several photographs of his uncle dressed as a woman. Lipstick. Dresses. When he showed them to me, I was reminded, yet again, of how appearances cannot be trusted. I also had to wonder, *Are these pictures of Sara?*

One thing that was working in the hotel's favor, oddly, was its dark past. A niche group of guests was curious about the criminal figures who'd stayed at the Cecil. "Did Richard Ramirez really stay here?" they would ask. There was a famous Austrian serial killer who was asked about just as frequently. Sometimes people from Austria would stay with us just for this reason. Many of the guests who were attracted to the sordid history of the Cecil were equally fascinated with the idea of it being haunted. They wondered if the ghosts of these killers were still roaming the halls.

"Is this a haunted hotel?"

This was a very popular question at the front desk. Mostly, people asked it at the Cecil, but anyone who was paying close attention asked it at Stay, because, after all, it was in the same building. "A hotel within a hotel" was how Steve once described it.

Haunted hotels are an entire subsect of the hospitality industry, because some people like to be a little scared. This is different, though, from being truly scared. Nobody wanted to hear about the deaths that had happened recently. They wanted the type of fear you get on a ride at Disneyland.

Whenever I was asked if the hotel was haunted, I'd smile and do my best not to engage. "I wouldn't know," I'd say, or, "Not as far as I can tell." I was glad that the haunted personality of the hotel turned out to be a positive, because so many other aspects of it were inescapably bad. Would we ever get central air installed? Or a new elevator bank?

The hope was that if we won the lawsuit with the city, then all of these changes would become possible, and the Cecil could finally meet its amazing potential. In the press release issued by *Downtown News* in July 2008, there is a section called "Future Plans." Here, some of Steve's ideas are laid out. He hoped to turn the Cecil's upper floors into a budget-friendly hotel, "but that will depend largely on the outcome of the lawsuit."

On paper, he seemed to understand the need to hold off on any big plans until the lawsuit was resolved. But in actuality, he was continuing to run wild with new concepts, and he had the freedom to run far. The owners gave Steve a lot of power and didn't do a great job checking in on his day-to-day affairs. One good reason for this was that all their energy was going into fighting the lawsuit that would either make or break their investment.

It would turn out later that Steve's plan to open new locations of Stay had never been communicated to the owners, and the trips and plans of expansion were plans he kept to himself. His focus on expansion was questionable, given that we were such a new company. He was being paid to oversee one building, not to check out real estate elsewhere. At the time, I clocked Steve's behavior as presumptuous rather than malicious. I just thought he was getting ahead of himself. The fact that the City of LA lawsuit was still pending meant that no one had a clear idea of what would happen in the future.

Later, Steve's decisions became more obviously sketchy to me. He dramatically reduced the staff and moved off-site, into an office in Pershing Square, where he installed a team for his future vision of expansion. This included a chef for the soon-to-be restaurant Tuck, the same chef would also travel to Honolulu for the "new restaurant that would open there," which was confusing for a few reasons. First, neither restaurant was close to opening, and second, does a chef need an office when there isn't an active opening plan? Another new hire was a lawyer who also happened to be a friend of Cindy's from college. Did we need legal counsel? No. Did the lawyer have a license to practice in California? No. Both the lawyer and the chef were raking in salaries that ranged from $90,000 to well over $100,000 per year, which had not been approved by the owners, and, to put the icing on top of this strange and morally corrupt cake, Steve also allowed the lawyer to live in the penthouse for free—with her two cats.

The penthouse was the size of five Cecil rooms, and its views were stunning. Sometimes, when we kept the art gallery open late for Art Walk, I would stay up there for the night. It wasn't exactly luxurious, but it was definitely a convenient place to stay for anyone who'd moved in from out of town, which is what Steve's lawyer friend had done.

Steve and Cindy also offered a room free of charge to their house-keeper Wendy, who had allegedly run into money troubles and had nowhere to go. Wendy was in her fifties, a large woman who lum-bered around very slowly. The way she walked suggested that she was carrying enormous burdens. She spent a lot of time at the com-plimentary iMac computers in the lobby. I didn't know much about her beyond the fact that she liked the internet and worked as a housekeeper. We'd smile at each other when she walked by the front desk, but we didn't talk very often.

Wendy moved in during a slow period, so it didn't feel like such a big deal that we'd given her a free room. But once Stay got so busy that we were having to turn guests away, it no longer seemed fair that Wendy was living in one of our high-demand rooms for free. I brought this to the attention of Cindy and Steve, who said it would be fine to offer Wendy a shared bunk room, which cost only $35 a night. When I presented this to Wendy, she didn't hesitate. She just said yes.

After she became a paying customer, I saw Wendy on the free

iMac computers less and less frequently. On the rare occasions that I did run into her in the lobby, she appeared to be sweating profusely. I assumed that it was due to the financial stress she was under. Often, she didn't pay us on time for her bunk room, and we would have to follow up, which created extra work. I got the feeling that Wendy was embarrassed about her situation, and I felt bad for her, but I wasn't sure how to help her—and I had absolutely no clue how badly she needed help.

On Valentine's Day 2010, I went to Disneyland with my then-boyfriend, Matteo. While we were there, my phone rang. I saw that it was the Cecil and thought, *What now?*

Lupe, who was the front desk supervisor at that time, delivered the news.

"Wendy has been found dead and it looks like an overdose. Pills, probably."

This news was hard to process and even harder to deliver to Cindy and Steve. I knew that Cindy, in particular, was going to be deeply upset, which of course she was.

The day after Wendy's death, I returned to work and got a call from her sister, who told me that she planned to come down from San Francisco soon to retrieve Wendy's belongings. She asked me what kind of condition Wendy's room was in, and I told her I didn't know. The coroner had sealed it off. I explained that legally, if she wanted me to break the seal, she would, as Wendy's family member, have to give me authorization. I have always taken rules seriously, and the coroner seal was no different.

"I'm giving you authorization," she said.

After we got off the phone, I asked Pedro to go check the room before I went in. He's a lot less squeamish than I am. He came back and reported that he saw a little bit of blood on Wendy's pillow. Other than that, her room appeared to be very clean and organized.

The next day, Wendy's sister arrived. In the elevator on the way up to Wendy's room, she said, "My sister tried to end her life before. And now she finally succeeded." Her sister also told me that Wendy had suffered from mental illness for many years, and that during the periods when she felt more content, she tended to stop taking her meds. Well, this was how Wendy had killed herself. She'd saved all the meds and then taken them at once. So if she had been feeling better, then it wasn't for long.

I left Wendy's sister alone in the room to give her some privacy and pack up whatever she wanted. After she was done, she told me we could throw away what was left in the room, and then she flew back to San Francisco. I thought it was the last time I was ever going to talk to her. But a couple of days later, she called me.

"I found a note in one of Wendy's coat pockets," she said. "It says she left a bag with the front desk."

This information sent chills down my spine. Not only had Wendy planned her death, but she had also packed a bag for her sister to find after the note was discovered. According to the note, the bag contained Wendy's most meaningful mementos, and many of them were family-related.

I remember going to the storage closet where we kept guests' luggage when they were waiting to check in or out. It was meant to house bags only on a very temporary basis, like a few hours at most. I wondered what Wendy had said to the front desk agent when she'd handed over the bag, and why nobody had flagged the bag, which hadn't been retrieved, because we were pretty strict about not keeping any luggage back there for too long.

I found Wendy's bag easily in the storage closet. It was the only one there, and it was enormous. I uneasily rolled the gigantic and heavy bag back to my office and left it sitting there for a few days, because that's how long it was going to take Wendy's sister to come back down from San Francisco. During those few days, it was an elephant in the room. Every time I looked at it, I imagined Wendy packing it and zipping it up. I imagined how depressed she must have been and how lonely she must have felt. If somebody had stepped up to pay her $35-a-day fee for staying at the hotel, would that have prevented her from killing herself? Or was it not that simple?

CHAPTER 8

The Verdict

Here's how the verdict of the lawsuit with the City of LA was explained to me: "They split the baby."

What this meant was that in the end, the owners still owned the entire building, but 301 rooms were designated as monthly rentals (and would remain designated as such, even if the rooms were never rented out again), and 299 of the rooms could be used as a hotel.

The other major part of the verdict was that because of the residential element, no major construction would ever be allowed. This meant that no new bathrooms would ever be added, a new elevator bank would never be installed, and central air and central heat were out of the question. This last detail was an extra problem, because technically, heat is a basic right of all tenants. So, after the verdict, we gave every tenant in the building temporary electric heaters.

The address of the original Cecil—640 South Main Street—and Stay's address continued to belong to the hotel's owners, but how half the building was going to operate would change. As I mentioned earlier, Stay consisted of 138 rooms on floors four, five, and six. The eighty or so remaining tenants lived on floors two and three. This meant that the rooms on all the other floors would need to be divided.

First, let me explain that even though 301 rooms were designated as residential, that didn't mean that we were required to fill them with new tenants after the current tenants left or passed away. We could leave them empty instead, and so that's what we did. Our remaining 299 rooms had a higher chance of being profitable if we weren't dealing with the issue of mixing our hotel population with the tenant population.

We had already decided that we would not be accepting new tenants, so we designated almost all of the sink-only rooms, because those were the least valuable. The long-term plan was to wait until all the tenants moved out or passed away, at which point we would no longer have the problem of mixing populations—but there were a few problems with this plan. First, it would probably take many years for all the tenants to vacate their rooms. And second, when and if that did happen, we'd still only have half a building to use as a hotel—and one that lacked the most basic amenities of central air and heat.

It was tragic and frustrating that such a large portion of the Cecil was going to go completely unused, but it was also the only option. Inviting more tenants into the building was not only at odds with the hotel plan; it was also, on its own, not profitable. The monthly rent varied according to how long the tenant had been there, but in general, it wasn't high. How much could we charge for run-down rooms, many of which offered shared bathrooms? Not that much.

The verdict of the lawsuit was dramatic, but it didn't really impact our everyday lives. We continued to run Stay, just as we'd been doing. The tenants continued to live at the Cecil. One small change was that the housing department stopped by more frequently to check that all the rooms designated for tenants were, in fact, empty. (They didn't want us double-dipping.) Beyond that, the shift that occurred after the lawsuit was probably mostly one of morale, because all the dreams of the Cecil ever becoming a profitable budget hotel were immediately slashed. From a financial perspective, the verdict really wasn't survivable. This was when it started to feel to me like the *Titanic* was sinking. Where else was there to go but down? After the lawsuit, we were treading water. How long could we go on doing that? To make matters more complicated, I was really the only one who was privy to this information, which felt isolating.

This doomed fate turned into a background whisper as time went on, which was understandable. There were so many problems screaming for my attention every day that it was easy to forget about our looming fate. At some point, we'd crash into the iceberg. For the time being, I was busily running around, putting out one fire after another. I guess you could say all the energy I exerted felt a lot like treading water.

Even though our bright future was gone, I continued touring groups as if it weren't. "And look at this view!" I'd say on the rooftop. During one tour, a woman who'd come on behalf of a rehab facility looked down at the folks in the Cecil lobby and told me that I should take a self-defense class, just in case.

"To protect myself against the tenants?" I asked.

"Yes," she said.

This is a good example of how difficult it was to sell a bright future, given the reality of the Cecil.

Still, we did have some success farming out our business to organizations. Movie scouts came by frequently asking if they could see the place, and sometimes they used it. This provided a nice little side income for the Cecil, although it was by no means a financial problem solver.

Members of various organizations moved in at different times. For a while, a group of students lived with us. During another period, we hosted a large population of Mennonites. Even though we charged these organizations less than we charged hotel patrons, it was preferable to keep the rooms filled and the money flowing in. This kept Stay afloat, but unfortunately, we never again enjoyed the popularity that we'd had in the beginning. The reviews were mixed, and reading them drove me crazy, so I stopped.

One of the things I always loved about my job at the Cecil was that it never slowed down. The pace was constant and fast, which really suited my personality. In those first few years, there was movement in my life away from the hotel, too. I moved from Hermosa Beach to West Hollywood, thinking that reducing my commute by eleven miles would make it faster. Unfortunately, my commute remained exactly the same, but it was still nice to be in a new environment.

The other major thing that happened during this period was that I took my first solo international trip. It was actually inspired by Steve, who told me I'd been working too hard and needed a break. So I went to Thailand. Travel has always offered me a welcome sense of perspective, and while I was there, I remember reflecting on my life and thinking, *Wow, this is going really well now.*

A few years earlier, I'd been working at a job I didn't love and dating the wrong guy. Now, I was working in an entirely different industry and I was thriving. Even though I was happy to be on vacation, I sort of missed the cast of characters at the Cecil. I suppose that in a way, it was a mutually beneficial relationship. They needed me, and I had started to need them, too.

CHAPTER 9

GM

In 2010, during a routine team meeting, Steve officially promoted me to the position of general manager. The way he framed it was as a side note, and I suppose that's how it felt to me, too. Nobody in the room was surprised. There was no big party. I'd already been doing most of the work that a general manager would do, and now I was finally getting the title.

And the office. That was exciting to me, because the general manager's office at the Cecil was, as I mentioned earlier, gorgeous, and ostentatious in an '80s way. I loved it. In my previous working life, I'd always been in a cubicle. This was the first time I had a key and a door I could close.

In the office, I had an elaborate oval-shaped wooden desk, probably ten feet long. Behind my chair, there was a glorious credenza. I also had an enormous conference table made of glass, a wet bar with a sink, a minifridge, and my own bathroom, complete with marble flooring. It definitely felt like an upgrade—until I looked out the window and saw the shady things that were happening in the alley. Constantly, there were people having sex, shooting up, and climbing in and out of the dumpster. It was sad and horrifying and dark—and also weird to watch from my over-the-top office.

In my new role, I became more familiar with the financial workings of the hotel. I started managing payroll and looking at profit-and-loss statements, which were never good. We were always hovering just above the red. Even when we did well, the expenses of the building canceled out our profit. This was when I started to realize how truly hopeless the future of the hotel was. I continued to steer the ship with enthusiasm anyway, knowing that at some point, it would end.

Along with our financial chaos, there was the chaos of daily life at the Cecil. At every moment, something seemed to be going wrong. Even the peaceful times were marked by strange drama. By the time I became general manager, it was second nature to me to call the cops whenever things went wrong, which was often. I must have dialed 911 at least once a week, if not more. What I'd also become accustomed to was how long it took the cops to show up when you were calling them from the Cecil. Sometimes it would take hours for them to arrive, because there just weren't enough officers to handle all the crime that was happening in the area. A lot of the time, I had to dial 911 several times before an operator answered. I quickly learned that a way to entice them to send help was to make the disaster seem imminent by saying something like, "I am in danger *right now*." Otherwise, it could take a very long time for someone to come—or they just wouldn't come at all. It was a disappointment to find out how broken and ineffective our system could be.

One day, a front desk agent called me after hours and said, "A guest jumped from a window and landed on the parking gate."

The gate they were referring to had barbed wire at the top. It was the same one I drove through every morning.

"The body's in the alley," the front desk agent said. "They're coming to remove it."

I remember feeling somewhat relieved that it was there as opposed to being in front of the hotel. This was still in the early days, when I thought we might actually have a chance at changing the Cecil's reputation.

What I learned after the body had been removed could be added to the long list of things I had never even thought to consider. When officials remove a body, they remove only the body, and not the rest. The next morning as I drove through the gate, I saw evidence of the anonymous jumper's death on the cement.

The other thing I'd never considered was who cleans up the mess. Well, in this case, a houseman was sent outside with a hose. I still think about how horrific this task must have been for him—and for all the employees who'd had to deal with this type of gore. How could cleaning up brain matter possibly be the job of someone who was making a pretty low minimum wage at a hotel? It just seemed wrong to me. It always amazed me how the staff would not only do what we asked of them but also with a smile. I honestly believe they were grateful to be there and have a job.

I should mention, too, that this death occurred during the time when the German rock band was living in the storefront of the hotel as part of a marketing ploy to create buzz. Johannes, a member of the band, who would remain my friend, told me that he and some of the bandmates had been up late partying the night before, and they had seen the anonymous man jump.

I never learned more about the identity of the man, or, if I did, I can't remember anything about him, which speaks to how common death was at the Cecil. I suppose that before this, when somebody killed themselves, I always thought about the family and friends who were affected. What I didn't think about were the strangers: the officials who came to collect the body, the houseman with the hose, and the members of the German rock band who had happened to see the final landing.

Mostly, I called the cops because people were behaving in a disorderly way. They'd yell, damage property, and sometimes become violent. The cops would show up to take them away—or they would not show up. And then another disturbance would occur, and then another, and then another. I frequently hear myself saying, "So many crazy things happened at that job." Here are a few examples to show you what I mean:

There was the dead snake we found in a bathtub, and the housekeeper who had sex with another employee on their lunch break, which was filmed by a third employee, another housekeeper, who smugly showed me the footage. I terminated these employees immediately, even though, according to them, they'd done nothing wrong because they'd been on lunch break. Later, I'd also terminate the second housekeeper because she was caught using a fake social security number.

Once, we found a portable counterfeit money machine in a room. Another time, a tenant told me that sex in the alley with a prostitute could go for as low as the price of a cheeseburger Happy Meal. And another time, a DEA agent showed up wanting to check the registration cards of everyone who was staying at the hotel. I remember watching him look at one card after the next. Eventually, he left without making a positive identification, so I assumed the perpetrator he was looking for was staying elsewhere.

Helping law enforcement officials do their job became a normal part of my working life. Once, a few members of the police department asked if they could use our rooms to lure potential child predators to meet "dates." They'd post ads on Craigslist, pretending to be underage, and then when the perpetrators showed up, they'd be arrested. The only reason I agreed to this was because they took the criminals down the back stairs and out the back door and not the front. Another time, two cops showed up and told me that they'd shot a man who was out of control running around on the 110 freeway. It turned out that he was a guest. Nobody ever came to collect his belongings, which happened all too often when our guests died.

Sometimes nice things happened. A former guest who got sober after staying with us returned to the hotel to make amends for how he'd damaged our property. In 2010, we hosted a large number of sober alcoholics from Alcoholics Anonymous and reminisced about how the Cecil was featured on the cover of a 1986 pamphlet called "How A.A. Came to Los Angeles." Inside this pamphlet, there's the story of how the first A.A. meeting in Los Angeles took place on a Friday night at eight p.m. inside the Cecil Hotel. According to an alcoholic named Mort J, the location was chosen "because the price was right and there was a good psychological reason for holding a meeting down there because I knew it would show us where we were headed unless we did something about it—that was our destination, Skid Row, the drunk tank, sleeping in the alleys and under the bridges, winos, dead men."

Within the framework of all the unexpected events at the Cecil, there was a definite routine. I'd show up every morning and sit at my humungous desk and check the numbers. Every day at three, I'd meet up with Pedro to chat and take a break. Frequently, I'd call the cops, hoping they would come. And every Friday morning, I'd walk over to the flower mart to pick up some bouquets for my home. They were gorgeous and cheap.

On July 16, 2010, that's what I was doing when I saw that I'd missed twenty-one calls from my sister. When I called her back, she said, "Dad's died."

What? Our dad was dead?

I was completely rattled. He'd died suddenly, of a stomach aneurysm, alone in his house.

I flew back to Michigan and made all the funeral arrangements with my sister. While I was away, I called the hotel and was told that Pedro had gone to the hospital because there was something wrong with his heart. He turned out to be okay, and I was so grateful, because it felt like way too much to handle.

During my trip to Michigan, and after, too, I thought a lot about how proud my dad was when I'd become the general manager of the Cecil. He was a blue-collar guy; he'd worked as a master plumber all his life. Often, when we talked on the phone, he'd say, "I'm going to make it out to LA soon to see where you work and what you are doing over there."

My dad had always meant to book that trip, but he never did, and then time ran out. After he died, I felt incredibly sad that he'd never see the place that had become such a big part of my life. I am not sure he would have really understood it, though. After all, he hated big cities.

CHAPTER 10

Sketchy Behavior

The tension among Steve, Cindy, and me was rising. During my trip to Michigan for my dad's funeral, they were on a planned vacation to Europe. Their lawyer friend who was living in the penthouse for free with her cats had been asked to step in and help while we were all away. When I returned, I learned that she hadn't reported to work, not even once. Apparently, she'd stopped by the front desk on her way out to see if everything was okay and that was it. I can't remember too many days at the Cecil where things just went off without a hitch.

When Cindy and Steve came back from their vacation, I had a sit-down conversation with Cindy. I told her that I felt uncomfortable with the dynamics at work. The lawyer was a college friend of Cindy's, and between Steve's seemingly unnecessary recent hires and the fact that the lawyer was living in the penthouse, I thought it was having a negative impact on our friendship. Then I presented her with a solution: "I think it would be best if we didn't talk about work at all." Looking back, this was more like avoidance than an actual solution, but it was the best I could do at the time. Things just didn't feel right anymore, and it was too uncomfortable to explain to Cindy.

Amazingly, some of Steve's expansion dreams did come true. Stay opened a second location in Honolulu. When it needed beds and other pieces of furniture, Steve had a truck show up to collect them from our property downtown. He wanted to ship it to Hawaii—and he did. I was asked to sign a bill of lading of the furniture that was being removed from the hotel, and I knew that was a legal document. Some of the furniture, like the beds, for example, we needed for the hotel.

Even though this was very clearly a problematic thing to do, I signed the papers and didn't stop Steve because I didn't want to be a rat. Instead, I quietly began keeping track of everything he'd taken from the property. I knew that at some point, the owners would figure out what was going on, and that's exactly what happened. One day, one of the owners approached me in the lobby and said, "I want to talk to you about some numbers." I was ready. I handed over the spreadsheet I'd been making and told him everything.

Ironically, Steve got fired on my birthday, August 26, 2011. It happened unceremoniously, on the phone. He was in Hawaii at the time, realizing his dreams of expansion. After the owners found out about his unapproved dealings in Honolulu, they uncovered that he'd been taking astronomical sums out of the hotel budget to pay himself, as well as his lawyer friend and multiple chefs. He'd also, it turned out, used the hotel's money to pay his own legal fees for his divorce. I hadn't known that, but I was familiar with his divorce status, because Steve involved me in it by requesting that I, his good friend and coworker, serve his ex-wife with the papers. Also, throughout his divorce proceedings, I let him borrow my car to take to the courthouse, because his Maserati was still in the shop. It's hard to get to Orange County without a car.

The owners could have taken legal action, but they decided that just moving on would be the more painless way to go. I was notified that Steve had been terminated and that he wasn't allowed on the property.

Then the text messages from Cindy started pouring in, and they were horrible.

Here's one I remember:

Die bitch!

This was my alleged best friend, and it was my birthday. I was devastated.

I celebrated my birthday with my mom and my godmother, who were visiting LA. The plan for the following day was that I'd drive them downtown with me and they could walk around and shop while I worked. This was their routine whenever my mom and godmother would visit. They got a kick out of shopping around Santee Alley and loved looking at all the counterfeit purses and fake MAC makeup.

Well, the next morning, before we got into the car, I received a call from a security guard, who told me that Steve was not only in the building but outside my locked office door waiting to see me. I was extremely anxious as I drove to the hotel. Steve wasn't supposed to be on the property, and he had a history of being volatile. What was he going to say to me?

Outside my office, I found Steve, who appeared to be seething.

"Hey, Steve!" I said in a lighthearted way. My mom and godmother were right behind me, which made me feel safer.

Steve grunted hellos to all of us, and I unlocked the door. Then he followed me into the office and slammed the door shut behind him. Well, after that, either my mother or godmother cracked the door open just a little and reminded Steve that they were right outside and could hear everything.

Steve ignored them and started telling me all the things he'd come there to say.

"I've been wanting to fire you for years," he claimed, even though he'd appointed me as general manager not long before. "And today, I'm finally doing it. You're fired." It sounded much like good old Donald on *The Apprentice*.

This made no sense. How did Steve, who'd just been fired himself, have the power to fire me?

He didn't, but that morning, I played along. It was easier than fighting with him. When he said, "You can collect your things and leave," I did just that. I loaded a bunch of my personal belongings (I'd acquired a lot over the years) onto a bell cart and rolled it down to the parking lot. Once we'd loaded everything into my car, we got in and I told my mom and godmother to zip it until we got back to my place. It was a whole lot to process, and even though I was pretty sure it was all temporary, there was a part of me that was worried.

When I got home, I called one of the owners and told him what had happened. The owner had Steve removed from the building and told me to take the rest of the day off. I don't know why I didn't listen to him. I guess it was because I didn't want anyone at work to be confused. I wanted them to see that I was still their leader, and that I was going to show up for them.

Shortly after Steve got fired, he sent Stay a cease and desist order that claimed we could no longer use the name Stay for our hotel. Secretly, he had trademarked the Stay concept and the name. Even though it seemed wildly unfair that Steve would walk away with anything, he got to keep the name and we had to change ours. This was when Stay became Stay on Main.

I thought there was a good chance that Steve would never come to the hotel again, but that turned out to be wrong. A few weeks after getting fired, he crept in one night and stole the fiberglass dog. He then brought it to the lobby of Stay Honolulu, where it still resides today.

CHAPTER 11

Missing

My relationship with Steve and Cindy dissolved immediately after Steve was fired. I continued to receive mean text messages from Cindy for a while. At one point, I walked to the police station to file a restraining order. They explained to me that the restraining order would remain on her record, and after learning that, I felt too guilty filing one. I didn't want Cindy to have a record. Eventually, her calls and texts faded and stopped altogether. The group of women we used to drink wine with were all caught up in the drama, and eventually it felt easier for me to just move on. Before I knew it, many of the people I'd spent a lot of time with had disappeared.

Things at the Cecil continued to be rocky. It's probably not that surprising, given the instability of the environment, that its ownership changed several times while I was there. Each time it sold was a different era. For the first year or so, the owner was South Main Street Partners, the group that claimed it had not known that the hotel was designated as a residential facility. For me, this was the most exciting period. I was thirty-two years old. I was working with my best friend as a designer. It was all so new and exciting, and the hope that we were going to be a successful version of the *Titanic* was alive and well.

Then the next era began. The Cecil was owned by the bank in 2010 along with Clive Fargo. Clive Fargo was one of the original investors. He owned the property with the lender and would also oversee the hotel operations and create new plans. The future didn't seem good, and I felt uncertain and uncomfortable a lot of the time. This period, for me, was when hope became harder to access. It was also the period during which I entered into a relationship—with Clive Fargo.

My first impression of Clive was that he was handsome and smelled like fresh soap. He was sixteen years older than me, and he had a big job and a fancy car. He began to invite me to political events, and I said yes. I was very apprehensive about dating him. I had never dated anyone older, and he certainly was older. We also ended up doing some side business together: Clive had seen what I'd done to revamp Stay and asked me to redesign the interior of his mom's condo in Irvine. Later, I did his dad's condo in Santa Monica. Clive was so impressed with my work that he bought three more condos in the same complex and I redesigned those. I completed those jobs on the weekends, since I didn't see Clive then anyway. He was with his kids.

Clive was a confusing guy, and why I was attracted to him wasn't exactly logical to me. I felt a strange mix of emotions when I was with him. On the one hand, it was familiar. On the other hand, I never felt at ease, or maybe I always knew it was never going to last. Emotionally, Clive was basically absent. With money, he was conflicted. Although he was wealthy, he often talked about how little money he had. There always seemed to be the fear that he could run out of it at any second. I'm not sure how much he really paid me for redesigning the three condos in Santa Monica, although I do believe he reimbursed me for the materials I'd purchased on my credit card. He used to jokingly call me "the bank of Amy Price." It was a lot like when I first started working at the Cecil, I suppose. I was just so happy to be using my creative skills that I thought, *Sure, I'll shoulder the expenses. Why not?*

Outside of work, I was most focused on jewelry. Every night after work (when I wasn't with Clive), I came home, sat down at my table, and made jewelry. As a practice, it calmed me. It gave me something to do with my hands. It seemed so simple compared to my work at the Cecil. And I loved selling my jewelry, too. Seeing a customer get excited about a piece and then buy it filled my heart with pride. And yet, I never considered leaving the Cecil and making the jewelry business a full-time endeavor. First, it didn't seem logistically feasible. And second, I was deeply emotionally attached to the hotel. I felt almost matriarchal about my role there. I genuinely cared about the building and everyone who inhabited it, and this caring gave me a sense of purpose.

My empathetic nature, however, was not always useful in the other parts of my life. My shouldering the hotel's expenses for Steve and then for Clive speaks to how I would sometimes give too much away. I have a long history of not being that discerning when it comes to what I give away, particularly when it comes to money and men. Steve and Clive are just two examples of this.

I'm mentioning this for two reasons. The first is to foreshadow what would happen when my old rehab boyfriend, Teddy, returned.

And by "returned," I mean "got out of prison after many years." And the other reason is to point out an interesting juxtaposition. While I had been extremely naïve in my personal life, the Cecil made me a lot less naïve about the world at large.

Five years into the job, I could handle charged situations with relative ease. If somebody screamed in the lobby or ran through it naked, it was sort of surprising, but it wasn't a total shock anymore. A glass bottle was thrown at my head one day (by a woman named Lauren Sanford; you'll be hearing more about her later), and after that, I came to expect having objects hurled at me. Because mental illness affected so many people who stayed at the hotel, it was expected that they'd exhibit odd and sometimes irrational behavior. There were many, many people whose bizarre antics were far more outlandish than Elisa Lam's.

If you've seen the Netflix documentary or remember this as a news story, then you'll be familiar with the facts of the Elisa Lam case. What I want to do is paint a picture of what happened from my point of view. The first time I ever heard Elisa's name, it was because an employee who was working at the front desk told me that a guest had complained about her.

"Amy, a woman in 506 is leaving Post-it notes on other guests' beds that say things like, 'Go Home.'"

Room 506 was the female dorm that contained six bunk beds. This and the male dorm were the cheapest rooms at the hotel, ideal for people on a tight budget. The front desk agent went on to tell me that there had been other complaints about Elisa from her fellow bunkers in room 506. Apparently, she had locked the door to the room several times and was asking people for a password in order to enter.

When I heard about these problems, my solution was to relocate Elisa. It was the end of January, and not that busy, so we had available rooms. She was offered her own room, and shortly after that, she moved. I expected that this would deter her from continuing to be disruptive, which it did.

Then, on February 1, 2013, she was reported as missing.

I found out about this when a police officer showed up at the hotel and told me that Elisa hadn't called her parents, which she normally did regularly, and that they were worried. Elisa was twenty-one years old, from Canada, and unfamiliar with the area, the cop told me. I said what I always said to law enforcement: "Let us know if there's anything we can do." He left. I expected that that would be the end of it.

But it was far from the end. The story quickly got a ton of attention from the press. Pictures of Elisa were all over the news and all over the neighborhood. Everyone wanted to know where she'd gone. After Elisa became a topic of conversation, an employee shared another story about her. Apparently, one day, she'd run into the lobby and screamed, "LA is crazy! And so am I!" And then she ran off. Maybe in a different setting, this outburst would have been alarming, but at the Cecil, it barely made a dent. I assumed that she was an odd woman who was prone to doing odd things. That was it. I didn't think anything of it until the police returned. They wanted to review our video footage.

Since we were barely making a profit, we couldn't afford things like new video cameras at the Cecil, so the footage was shoddy. The cameras had probably been installed in the 1980s. It was amazing they filmed anything at all. I set the officers up in a room to watch the footage. They worked tirelessly for days on end. Eventually, they found some footage of Elisa in the elevator. When the investigators actually located her on camera, it was big news to all of us. I had been working with them on a daily basis. I remember one of them saying, "We found her."

The few minutes that had been filmed were strange. Elisa walked in, pressed the buttons for every floor, but the door didn't close. She stuck her head out of the elevator door and looked both ways, and then hid in the corner as if she was suspicious. I wouldn't see any of this in full until much later. At the time, all I knew was that one of the officers asked me, "Where does the trash go out?"

I told them where, and then I asked them why they were asking me that question. And that's when they explained to me that according to the video footage, Elisa hadn't left the hotel. Their working theory was that maybe she'd been killed and hauled out in trash bags.

During this time, another story about Elisa emerged. According to an employee who was working at the front desk, Elisa called and asked for some coke. A few months earlier, Clive had sent Pedro and me to buy a soda machine he'd seen on Craigslist. When we got there, the guy who was selling it told us that he also had a vending machine for frozen items for sale. Unexpectedly, I bought it. Then, instead of ice cream, I bought a bunch of snacks that I thought people would like, including frozen pizzas and Hot Pockets (we provided guests with a microwave), and I installed my vending machine in the lobby, right next to Clive's soda machine. Mine wasn't as much of a money-maker, but it certainly felt fun to own my own vending machine.

So when Elisa called asking for coke, the employee told her to come down to the lobby and buy one. Allegedly, according to that employee, Elisa said that wasn't the type of coke she was looking for and hung up.

All of these stories about Elisa were relayed to the police officers. Then they started questioning all of the employees. It was a
scary time, especially for the unauthorized immigrants who were
working for us. That was never something I asked about, but it was
understood that there was a large possibility that not everyone was a
legal citizen of the US. After I saw ICE come in and take one of our
employees away, the consequences of not having citizenship were
starkly apparent to me, and I understood why people were scared.
All of our employees were questioned, which brought to light no new
information. Meanwhile, days were passing. If Elisa hadn't left the
hotel, then where had she gone?

The cops, who were understaffed, because a lot of them left our
case to work on the police killer case that was huge at that time,
brought in dogs to search for Elisa's scent. One of the dogs followed
it to a window that led to a fire escape. It was another dead end—or
so we thought.

Desperate for information, the LAPD decided to put the video of
Elisa in the elevator on their website. The hope was that the public
would respond with some new information. This was where things
started going awry. The video went viral. Millions of people watched
it. Web sleuths set up channels dedicated to Elisa's disappearance.
They picked apart every detail. Why had she pressed the buttons for
every floor? Why had she looked out the door as if somebody was
following her? Was that a shoe next to her in the hall, or was that
just a splotch? Citizens became private detectives, and many theories
were spawned.

While the internet was blowing up, the LAPD found out that
Elisa was on medication, and that she had most likely stopped taking

it. They also learned that Elisa, off meds, was prone to paranoia, and also prone to hiding. Still, we couldn't find her anywhere in the hotel.

More time went by. The news vans started coming less frequently. The signs of Elisa all over downtown stopped looking so new. There was nothing else to be done. It felt like we might never find her. I thought I was going to catalogue Elisa Lam as yet another guest who went missing from the Cecil.

In early February, while the investigators were still conducting their search, Clive proposed to me in San Francisco on Valentine's Day. After that, I went on to the Tucson Gem and Mineral Show so I could buy stones, which I do every year. The combination of the jewelry show and becoming engaged meant that I was in a wonderful mood when I returned to work the following Monday.

On Tuesday, February 19, 2013, Pedro walked into my office at around ten a.m. with Santiago, one of the maintenance guys. I remember noting that Santiago looked petrified.

"Price," Pedro said, "we have a problem."

I could tell immediately that something was really wrong.

"The missing girl," he said, "is here."

"Where?" I asked.

"The tank."

CHAPTER 12

Found

Guests had complained about the water pressure being low. That's why Santiago went up to the roof to check the tank. It wasn't out of the ordinary for this to happen. Sometimes there would be a clog that needed to be manually fixed. The tanks operated on the gravity system that includes a chain. From time to time, the chain would get caught.

When Pedro told me that Elisa was in the tank, I was shocked. Beyond shocked. It was almost too insane to comprehend. My mind was spinning. It took me a second to gather my thoughts, and then I said, "I'm going to deal with this. Can you shut the door on your way out, please?"

Pedro and Santiago left my office. For some reason, I had the impulse to go into the bathroom then. I sat on the toilet seat for a minute that felt like an hour, wondering how this had happened, and why, and what was going to happen next. I knew that everything was about to change.

As I mentioned earlier, I called my mother before I called the police. It was an impulse. The phone was ringing before I'd fully made the decision to call her. I think I just wanted to tell somebody who loved me what was going on. My mom was in Michigan, probably watching *Days of Our Lives* when I called. "Mom!" I was panicking. "They found the missing woman in the water tank!" I was speaking so fast that I'm not even sure my mother understood what I was saying.

After that I called Clive, who said, "I'm on my way." As an emotionally supportive partner, he was mostly useless, but I was grateful that he was coming.

Then I called one of the homicide detectives who'd camped out watching the video footage for days. He didn't answer. I called two or three more times, and then I finally dialed 911.

"You need to head over," I said. "The missing girl was just found here."

The police came fast. Within minutes, I could hear sirens. And then there were more sirens, and more sirens. It turned into an absolute mob scene very quickly.

Pedro took the cops up to the roof while I stayed downstairs navigating the additional crews of people that were coming in response to the call. Everyone in the lobby was confused. When guests asked me what was going on, I deflected. "We're figuring it out," I said, "and we'll know more soon." I didn't really know what else to tell them.

The most acute problem after Elisa had been found was our water supply. The health department was contacted either by me or the authorities. I really can't remember; there was just so much going on. A large number of officials showed up, maybe ten of them. I took them to my office and said, "We have a body in our drinking water, and we believe she's been there for nineteen days."

The health officials looked at me like I was kidding.

"There's a *real* body in your water tank?" one of them asked.

"Yes!" I said. "The body of the woman who's been missing."

Unsurprisingly, none of the health department officials had encountered this problem before. One of them actually said, "We've dealt with squirrels before, but not this."

The officials were led up to the roof to join the other officials. The fire department had already started to drain the tanks. This meant that four thousand gallons of water were drained onto Main Street that day. How far did it travel? I always wondered that.

Obviously, without water, we were forced to close down the hotel. What did we do with our guests? We relocated them to other hotels in the area. As for our tenants, some of them refused to leave. They just said no. So I asked an employee to go out and buy a bunch of bottled water. We put some of the bottles in the lobby for hotel guests to take with them on their way out, and we gave the rest to the tenants who wouldn't leave. We also asked them to sign a waiver that said they'd been asked to vacate the premises. Apparently, that was the legal requirement.

The guests were easy to relocate. They were tourists. All the hotels in the area were happy to take them in at our expense. As for the tenants who wanted to leave, it wasn't as easy finding them a place to go. I called half a dozen motels in the area and offered them my credit card number, but when I told them I was calling on behalf of the permanent residents of the Cecil, they all said, in various ways, "No thanks."

While I was making calls, one of the homicide detectives walked in. I was so relieved to see a friendly face. Both of us said, "I can't believe it." That's how everyone felt at the time. The fact that Elisa was in the water tank was just unbelievable.

"It's crazy," the detective said. "And the other day, I also received a very strange call about it . . ."

"Who called you?" I asked.

"A man who told me he was a clairvoyant. Calling from China."

"What did he say?"

"He told me, 'The girl is in the water.'"

"What?"

"I didn't have any idea what he was talking about until now."

"Oh my god, I have the chills," I said. "That's bizarre."

Whether it was a true vision or a coincidence seemed beside the point. How had the so-called clairvoyant pinpointed this tragedy so accurately?

Over the course of the afternoon, I had no luck finding any motels who were willing to take in our tenants. So after hours of trying, I got in my car and started driving around looking for a motel that would say yes. Maybe if they saw my face, it would be harder to reject me. I finally found a manager at a motel near the 110 who said, "Of course I'll take your money." I was overjoyed. And exhausted. After I'd arranged for the tenants to be transported over to that motel, I went home. It had been both the longest day ever and the shortest. It had gone by in a flash.

The next morning, I returned to the hotel. In order to be operational again, we had to get our water back, but it was complicated. A square hole had been cut in the tank to get Elisa's body out, which meant that it now needed to be repaired. That was going to take time.

We also had to get the tank cleaned, which was going to take time, too. After those tasks were completed, the water would have to be tested to make sure it was safe.

Meanwhile, we had to cancel all of our upcoming reservations. I wrote to the guests who'd booked on our website to apologize, and then I contacted our third-party partners, like Expedia, notifying them of the closure. The contacts I spoke with were people I had known for a long time, and they kept saying, "I'm sorry, Amy."

We also filed an insurance report, because we couldn't afford to pay for all the work that was being done on the roof and we certainly didn't have any revenue coming in until further notice. And then I was forced to start laying off employees. We were in dire straits financially, and without guests, there wasn't much for them to do. It was hard. The people who worked for us hadn't done anything wrong, and now they were going to be out of a job.

After almost everyone left, the hotel had a creepy feeling to it. It was literally dark because the lights were mostly off, and the phone would not stop ringing. The only remaining people were me, Pedro, a few other employees, and the ten or so tenants who'd refused to leave, and I think we were all asking the same questions.

What was going to happen next?

When would we recover from this tragedy?

Would we ever *fully* recover?

After the water tank was welded and refilled, the water testing began. We waited with great anticipation for the results. If the water was still contaminated after the refilling of the tank, it was going to be a big issue that could lead to more legal problems. The water test was more of a liability than a problem to fix. If it had been contaminated, then it could have affected our guests and tenants with potential health problems.

When the results came back negative, I was so thrilled. And so grateful. Uncontaminated water meant that we could reopen. It also meant that technically, the water was okay to drink, although after the tragedy, most of our employees refused to. They'd been emotionally traumatized.

Thankfully, insurance ended up covering our losses for the days we hadn't been operating. I don't know what we would have done otherwise. Without this little bit of help at the right time, we might have closed forever. But we survived, just as we'd survived so many other calamities before this one. Roughly three weeks after the day Pedro and Santiago came to my office with the news, we reopened.

CHAPTER 13

Tragedy Tourism

In the aftermath of Elisa's death, guests were stranger than usual.

Many people booked stays with us specifically because she'd died on the property. What could that have possibly meant if not that these guests wanted to be closer to her tragedy—and to the other tragedies of the past? Elisa's story dredged up the dark history of the Cecil very effectively. Suddenly, there was chatter about Richard Ramirez again, and the Austrian serial killer.

But booking a stay to be closer to tragedy paled in comparison to the weird performances spawned by Elisa's death. Once, I got a call from someone at the Pacific Electric Building telling me there was a man playing the guitar on top of one of the water tanks. It was ten o'clock at night. The man had risked his life to put on this show. He'd had to climb the fire escape up to the top of a 150-foot building, just as Elisa had most likely done.

Here is the note from the front desk:

At 4pm, the front desk received a phone call from one of the residents at the PE lofts indicating she was looking at a couple up on the rooftop. The man was playing a guitar and the woman was dancing on the water tanks. The resident recommended that we send security.

Another time, I was working in my office and I noticed movement out of the corner of my eye. When I turned to look, I saw a guy dangling from the fire escape ladder. He was trying and failing to climb the building. I named him Ninja Turtle.

We tried to stop trespassers from sneaking in, but it was hard to do efficiently. There were always so many people at the hotel, and we only had one security guard working at a time. Generally, security guards are hired to just stand there. The hope is that their mere existence will be enough to stop people from doing questionable things. The security guards at the Cecil were probably more involved than those at, say, Gap, but still, we didn't have enough of them to stop all the people who were attempting to sneak in.

Along with the performance artists mentioned above, there were graffiti artists. The art on the water tank changed often, even though the roof was a restricted area that you had to risk your life to get to. We also had amateur filmmakers trying to make their own movies.

Here's a note from the front desk about a reenactment of the Elisa Lam elevator video:

Security saw strange things on hotel security cameras. An Asian female with a bob cut wig, a red zip-up sweater/hoodie, some converse, and a skirt. She was being recorded by a Hispanic male who was wearing black pants, a camouflage jacket, and black running shoes. These individuals were re-enacting the Elisa Lam elevator scene.

They went into the same elevator, and the girl on video began to press all the buttons, and they ended up on the 15th floor. This is where the girl began to start acting the scene where Elisa Lam was peeking outside of the elevator doors and walking in and out of the elevator. There was a guest inside the elevator at the time. Security went up the 15th floor to check out the situation. He found 4–5 people in the 15th floor emergency escape stairwell. He kicked them out with a warning.

At 11pm, security found the same group in the back alley and asked them to leave. From the time that they were caught in the stairwell to the time they were caught in the alley, security stated that the group had tried to enter the building on three other occasions. I advised security to arrest them and call the cops if they were to catch them again. They have been told four times and they are still consistent in trying to access the building.

And here is another note:

At around 2pm, a trespasser was caught in the elevator. The guy seemed to be imitating Elisa Lam in the video. Security called the police, but when the cops arrived, they discovered that the suspect was under the age of 18.

Along with reenactments like this, there were civilian investigations and witchy demonstrations. I remember watching a video that had been posted on YouTube during this time. It showed a group holding a séance at the hotel.

People fascinated by the supernatural were calling the hotel constantly, or coming up to the front desk and asking questions about Elisa. Ghost hunters showed up, and psychics. It was amazing how many strangers had an opinion about this young woman's end. We received crank calls every day. I'd pick up the phone at the front desk anxiously because I never knew if the caller was going to be somebody with an earnest question or somebody who was entertaining themselves with practical jokes.

On a day-to-day basis, it was stressful dealing with all of these interlopers. And when I sat down and thought about what they were actually doing, it seemed incredibly sad to me. It felt as though the people making videos and other art about Elisa had forgotten the reality of her death, or they'd placed the importance of their own art-making above it. A tragedy had occurred. That's what had happened. The humanity of her story was lost in all of the dumb (and often dangerous) endeavors to sensationalize what had happened to her. Why did this particular story strike such a chord with people? Did it reflect their worst fears? Did it simply give curious folks something to do?

Many were captured by Elisa's story, and of course that included Hollywood. An episode of *American Horror Story* was very obviously based on her death. I was approached many times after that asking if it had been filmed on-site. The answer was no. But other things were filmed on-site. After Elisa's tragedy, there was an influx of film shoots that occurred at the hotel. *Castle*, *Basketball Wives*, and *Sons of Anarchy* are three that I can remember. We earned up to $15,000 a day per shoot, which was incredibly useful, given that we were, as always, sinking closer and closer to financial doom all the time.

Talk of money calls to mind the practical aspect of my job, which, during this period, was buried under mountains of hoopla.

Amid all the nutty situations that were constantly unfolding, I still had to manage a hotel and run a business. My responsibilities as the general manager of the Cecil were always wilder and more unexpected than they would have been at the vast majority of other hotels. If I'd worked at a Marriott in a quieter part of the city, for example, my job would have been more straightforward. At the Cecil, I was used to dealing with a lot of strange situations. What was new was that so many of them were focused on the death of a single person.

The other thing that happened in the aftermath of Elisa's death was that Stay on Main was no longer delineated from the Cecil. All the work we'd done to rebrand that section of the hotel disappeared, and we became known as the place where the girl was found dead in the water tank. Even now, this is how I sometimes explain the place where I used to work. If somebody hasn't heard of the Cecil, I say, "The hotel where the girl died in the water tank." Usually, this jogs people's memories. And if not, I add, "And the hotel that the Night Stalker, Richard Ramirez, allegedly called home about thirty years ago."

"Oh," people usually say. "Right. I know that one."

Eventually, we closed the Stay on Main lobby that we had worked so hard to build, because there no longer seemed to be a point to having separate lobbies, and we simply couldn't afford it. We could no longer hide from our reputation after Elisa. We didn't take down the sign that said Stay on Main, though, nor did we take away its rooms on floors four, five, and six. We continued to charge more for those rooms and offer a complimentary breakfast to the guests staying in them. Besides these small differences in options, the hotel was the same for all guests. Everyone entered and exited through the same doors.

It's worth noting that since I'd arrived at the Cecil in 2007, our prices had gone up and our protocol for checking in changed. After we started requiring a credit card number from guests at Stay, we implemented the same rules at the Cecil, as I mentioned earlier. So the days of people checking in with their trash bags were gone, or at least greatly diminished. This meant that there was less of a need to separate our Cecil guests from our Stay on Main guests. Over the years, the things that had separated them (money, class, background) dissolved. The coverage of the Elisa Lam story kind of finalized the breaking of the boundary between our two populations.

One thing the YouTube sleuths were particularly interested in was *how* Elisa died. Her body was found in February. The coroner's report wasn't released until June. This gave curious civilians a few months to come up with a wide array of conspiracy theories, which ranged from sort of plausible to totally deranged. Some people rejected the idea of suicide and decided it was a homicide. Some thought that I had killed her, or that the murderer was another hotel employee. There was a big controversy about whether or not the hatch on the water tank was open or closed when she was found. If it was closed, that meant murder. If it was open, then suicide or an accident seemed more possible.

In June, the coroner's report deemed Elisa's death accidental. The most popular (and, in my mind, the most plausible) chain of events goes like this: Elisa stopped taking her meds, which put her in a vulnerable position. At some point, she climbed out the window and onto the fire escape. This was where the cops' dogs had lost track of her smell. Given what her family had revealed about how she became paranoid and prone to hiding when she was off her meds, it would seem to follow that maybe she thought the water tank would be a good place to hide. What she didn't know (what she couldn't have known) was that once inside, it was almost impossible to get out.

In the fall of 2013, a few months after the coroner's report was released, Elisa Lam's parents sued the Cecil for wrongful death. They claimed the hotel was responsible for their daughter's tragedy. According to some rumors, people thought that I should have contacted social services after she had the outburst in the lobby, or after she locked other guests out of the shared dorm room. What those people didn't realize was that if I had called social services and reported these things, I highly doubt that they would have come. A big, ugly lesson I've learned from all my years working at the Cecil is that the resources we imagine are available to us often are not when it comes down to it. In a small town, maybe a social worker would have considered it an emergency. In downtown LA, right next to Skid Row, everything is an emergency.

Interestingly, it was after the Lams filed a lawsuit that our attorney called me and said, "The Lams have requested to be taken to the roof to see where their daughter died." He went on to explain that I was in no way obligated to show them.

"You don't have to do this, Amy," he said.

After a moment of thinking, I decided it would only be fair to grant the Lams' request. "Tell them I will do it," I said.

Shortly thereafter, the Lams showed up in the lobby with their attorneys. Our attorneys were also present. Together, we were a group of about ten people. I remember Pedro was standing close to me, and I remember how everyone started shaking hands and greeting one another. And I just stood there, watching, and waiting for someone to shake my hand, but no one did. It didn't exactly hurt my feelings. I understood the day wasn't about me or my comfort. But it didn't feel great, either. I had certainly never had been in a business meeting before where I was the only one that was excluded.

We rode up in two separate elevators. Pedro and I were in one with our lawyers, and the Lams were in the other with theirs. We took the elevator all the way to the highest floor and then walked up the short staircase to the roof. Pedro opened the door, and I led the group in the direction where the water tanks were located. There were four tanks on top of the Cecil. We led them directly to the one where Elisa was found. On the roof, Pedro and I stood off to the side, not knowing where else to go and also not wanting to disrupt them.

I'll never forget how Elisa's mom fell to the ground and started screaming. The pain she felt was palpable, and horrible, and I felt so badly for her. I remember an attorney kneeled down beside her and offered words of comfort. Elisa's dad, meanwhile, was as still as a statue. It was one of those scenes that was very difficult to take in. I felt so sad for the Lams. We had repaired the tank rather than buying a new one, so the hole that had been cut out to remove Elisa's body was still visible because it was easy to see where it had been patched and covered. I wondered if they noticed that or not.

Months later, I gave my deposition for the lawsuit, as did Santiago and Pedro. Eventually, the case was dismissed. The court ruled that we hadn't been at fault for Elisa's death, which was a relief.

I have thought a billion times about Elisa Lam going into the water tank and what it would have taken for her to get out. Being a very good swimmer myself, I know it would have taken a lot. As I said before, it was nearly impossible. She would have had to go all the way to the bottom, empty her lungs, and then spring up fast and shoot out of the water and grab the side of the open tank. There would not have been a ladder to grab since the tank is not designed for people to be on the inside. She must have been so scared when she realized she wasn't going to be able to do that. I imagine that she must have screamed, and despite the fact that there were hundreds of people in the building just below, nobody would have heard her. That's the part that I find most haunting.

CHAPTER 14

Trying to Move Forward

The only reasonable thing to do after Elisa's death was to keep moving. That's always been my default anyway: to go forward, and quickly.

Looking back, I can see that everyone who worked at the Cecil had been traumatized by what had happened. And I suppose that even then, I was aware of this to some degree. I found an organization to offer psychological support to our employees for free. None of them took advantage of this, including me. I think we were all in some sort of denial about how deeply we'd been affected.

Allowing the constant avalanche of work to cover over the rest of my life was, in many ways, a comfort. There was always something to do, always a fire to put out. I wasn't focused on myself, which was precisely the point. I didn't have to face my fears, artistic or otherwise, and with work in the way, it was easier to forget about how lonely I was after losing so many of my friends to Steve and Cindy. During this time, what sustained me was my friendship with Pedro and making jewelry. Clive might have sustained me to some degree, too, although that relationship was always complicated.

What Clive began talking about after Elisa's death was selling the hotel. We weren't meeting our financial marks, and he was getting pressure from the lender. The Band-Aid of Stay on Main had basically disintegrated. Our cool hostel concept definitely couldn't compete with the news stories about how many sad things had happened at the Cecil. And this was only one of the many factors working against us. There was no way to surmount the lack of bathrooms or the lack of air-conditioning. The fact remained that as long as just over half of the building was designated as being residential, a massive renovation was most likely never going to happen.

It was hard to watch the dreams that Cindy, Steve, and I had been so excited about in the beginning crumble. We were forced to close Marty, the coffee shop, because it was a drain financially. Arty stayed open a little bit longer, only because we kept the doors locked most of the time. The space essentially served as a window-shopping event to passersby.

You know how I said before that after the verdict of the lawsuit came in, I felt like the clock was ticking on the Cecil? Well, after Elisa Lam's death, it was ticking louder, and we were having an even harder time staying afloat than before, so it seemed a little bit ridiculous to continue to exert extra effort on the coffee shop and the gallery. Nip and Tuck had already died because of the no-construction clause. As I watched Marty close, and later Arty, it felt like our great big dreams for the Cecil were firmly in the past tense.

Around 2014, Clive succumbed to the lender's pressure and sold the hotel. This time, the buyer was Richard Born, a genius real estate developer based in New York, who had a history of revamping problematic buildings. For me, this period felt rejuvenating. Even though I knew about all the insurmountable issues of the hotel, I trusted that we were in good hands. And frankly, it was a relief that I would never have to hear Clive talk about his Cecil-related worries again.

Funnily, it was right after the sale to Richard Born that Clive and I called off the engagement. But it was one of those breakups that doesn't feel like a real breakup, because we sort of kept seeing each other. For years, we maintained a friendship that was slightly murky in nature. Sometimes we'd have "lunch" together. Even though we weren't romantically compatible, it was just one of those relationships that didn't die easily. The only real difference after we officially broke up was that I stopped wearing the engagement ring and imagining any real plans for the future.

When I wasn't at work, I traveled and continued to make and sell jewelry. I grew fond of taking international trips by myself, and during every vacation period, I went somewhere new. Vietnam, Israel, Cambodia, Indonesia, China, India, Nepal, Russia. I kept filling my passport with stamps. In every new place I visited, I bought precious stones and beautiful artwork and enjoyed the alone time. It was fortifying, and it helped me decompress from the stresses at work.

One thing that hadn't worked in the relationship with Clive was his dismissal of my jewelry-making dreams. He mirrored the fearful voice in my head that told me I was going to fail. Even though that was my fear, I kept moving forward with my business. At some point, I hired models to pose with my jewelry at El Matador Beach in Malibu, which was so exciting for me. I also kept participating in shows. It was a lot of work to prepare for those, and to install a table and set everything up, and then disassemble it all at the end of the day. Normally, I made just a little more than I'd spent on expenses to participate in the show. I would have liked to have earned tons of money, of course, but the thrill of just being there was intoxicating to me.

At the hotel, things continued to move forward in their usual dramatic way.

A good example of the tenant drama I was dealing with was Simon Bailey. He lived on the tenth floor, which was already a sign that he was a problem. Unlike his more cooperative peers, who'd moved downstairs to floors two and three, Simon refused. You might remember me mentioning the tenant who complained that he'd been locked out of the bathrooms and showers (this was not remotely true), which led to the stop work order, and then eventually to the years-long lawsuit between the owners and the City of LA.

Simon was the one who made that false claim.

A more notable fact about Simon Bailey: He was a convicted child molester. So "creep" is only the tip of the iceberg. I found it alarming to be in the presence of Simon. I'd seen the mug shots of confirmed pedophiles in the news, but I had never been in a situation where I was forced to interact with one. I was scared of him because of his criminal past, and because I knew he was a fan of lying his way into a lawsuit. I wasn't unfriendly with Simon, but I wasn't friendly, either. I was professional.

Simon was impossible to miss. He could most often be found sitting outside the hotel, selling prescription drugs. I called the police several times to try to get them to do something about this. They did nothing. So I eventually stopped calling.

The other thing Simon loved, aside from making money off pills, were young boys. Early on, I was told that if I ever saw Simon wearing a blond wig, that meant he was hunting. Simon took on different forms of blond. I wasn't quite sure how to read them. Sometimes he'd dye his own hair. Other times, he wore a hat with a fake blond mohawk attached to it.

Simon claimed that he used to be affiliated with a popular Motown band. I've forgotten which one now, and it doesn't really matter, but I'm bringing this up because I sort of believed that he had had success once. I assumed that before he'd been caught for molesting children, he'd lived a different life, one in which he wasn't seen as a pariah.

Sometimes the young boys who came up to Simon wanting to buy drugs didn't have enough money to do so. When that happened, Simon would bring them up to his room, maybe to accept payment in other forms. All of our security guards were aware of this issue and trained to check the IDs of anyone who looked remotely young. The ones who were over eighteen would stay for days, sometimes up to a week. They all looked malnourished. And Simon had many repeat visitors.

If you were to walk around the area of downtown LA where the Cecil is located, you'd see a lot of the same characters repeating the same routines. When Simon was around, it was often the same people buying drugs from him every week, and he had a large customer base. Once, while Pedro and I were out walking, he pointed at a woman and said, "I heard she gave Simon her child in exchange for drugs."

Was that true?

I have no idea, but I wouldn't be surprised if it was.

In addition to the Motown story, there were rumors about how Simon was a millionaire. He'd drop all sorts of names in an effort to impress people. But he'd lived at the hotel for about forty years.

I found it hard to imagine a millionaire was hiding at the Cecil, although any crazy thing could have been possible there.

Another major thing to know about Simon: he was very sick. Once a week, he was picked up by a van and taken to the hospital for dialysis. Many said he also had AIDS. Were these diagnoses connected to the large amounts of prescription drugs he seemed to be in possession of all the time?

Maybe, although I'll never be sure.

Over the years, Simon got weaker and weaker. At first he had a limp, and then he was rolling himself around in a wheelchair. He started to look really unhealthy. I didn't get the impression that he was a drug addict. He seemed more interested in the dealing side of things. I don't recall him ever being drunk, either. I never saw him in an altered state. He was, however, a very heavy smoker.

Sometimes, while Simon was at his weekly dialysis appointment, people would stop by the front desk and say things like, "I'm Simon's friend, and I need to go to his room to get something for him. I have his permission."

The stories were never that believable to me, and they all contained the same goal, which was to get into Simon's room when he wasn't there. A lot of these so-called friends seemed like drug addicts. I assumed they wanted to get into his room to steal his stash, and maybe also his millions of dollars.

One day, Simon went to the hospital and never returned. I realized that he was dead when the coroner called me asking me for the name and phone number of his emergency contact. When I went to open Simon's file, I saw that a brother was listed.

On this same day, the day I learned he was dead, a woman appeared at the front desk and tried to sweet-talk her way into Simon's room. The attempts to get in there just would not stop, even after he was gone.

I should probably mention that Simon's room was a nightmare, or a hoarder's paradise. From the floor to the ceiling, it was packed with stuff. He owned crates and crates of records, artwork, and thousands of VHS and DVD collection tapes. At least half of them were porn.

There was so much stuff in Simon's room that it was hard to walk from the door to his bed, which was also covered with stuff. He had a toilet in his room and, all around it, more stuff. A picture of Simon appears briefly in the Netflix docuseries, and in it, he is lying on his bed, surrounded by his mountains of things.

Not long after Simon died, I received a phone call from his brother—who was also named Simon. Simon explained to me that he and his other brothers had rented a truck in Texas and would be driving to Los Angeles soon to collect our Simon's stuff.

"There's a lot of pornography, just so you're prepared," I said.

"No problem," the brother said. "There are a lot of us."

A few days later, someone from the front desk came into my office and said, "Simon Bailey is here to see you." This was chilling considering that the only Simon Bailey I'd ever met until that point was dead.

When I went into the lobby, I found not one but four Simon Baileys waiting for me.

Yes, all of these brothers allegedly had the exact same name.

I did not know what to make of this. Were they telling the truth? More important, did it matter? I thought they looked related enough.

Their appearances were similar and so were their mannerisms. Also, if they wanted to remove the wreckage of Simon's room, I wasn't going to oppose that.

After the four Simon Baileys assessed the situation in the room, one of them came down to the lobby in a bathrobe and told me that loading the U-Haul was going to take them a while, so they'd be staying overnight . . . but they couldn't all fit in the same room.

"Okay . . ." I didn't understand how this could possibly be my problem.

Two of the brothers ended up staying in the room, and the other two stayed at a motel nearby. I didn't ask which one. I didn't care.

The next day, when I arrived at work, I found the two Simons who'd stayed in their brother's room overnight downstairs in the lobby watching TV. Both of them were wearing bathrobes and seemed very comfortable. Later, the other two Simons arrived. They also seemed to be in good spirits.

Meanwhile, one of the housemen reported seeing a brother with a large wad of cash. We'll never know exactly what was in that room, but for some reason this detail about the cash, like the detail about Motown, seemed possibly not incorrect. Was this why all the Simons seemed so happy? Because they'd found the secret money stash? Pedro definitely thought so.

Once the Simons were done, they told us that we could discard anything that had been left in the room. Pedro and I went up to check. When we opened the door, the clutter looked almost exactly the same as it had before the brothers arrived—with the exception that a lot of it was upside down, flipped on its side, or sitting askew. Basically, the room looked like it had been ransacked.

Before the brothers left, I told them that I would have to charge them a cleaning fee. "It's going to take a lot of work to remove that amount of property from the room," I said.

"We'll discuss it and call you," one of the Simons said.

Of course, I never heard from them.

During the weeks following Simon's death, people would come up to the front desk and say, "Is he really gone? I can't believe it."

Simon truly was a fixture outside the hotel, the unhealthy guy with the blond hair selling drugs to young boys out in the open, knowing he wouldn't be caught.

Another tenant, Kia Conroy, was in her early thirties, about five feet tall, and heavy. She wore outdated glasses and was missing a lot of teeth, which was hard to miss when she spoke. Her hair was very short, and she somehow appeared to be both meek and masculine at the same time. My impression was that Kia had probably not had the easiest time in life, and that she seemed sad about it. Even though she was in her thirties, she had a babyish quality that made her seem much younger.

Peter Conroy, Kia's father, was twice her age, about a foot taller, and always wore a baseball cap, a graphic T-shirt, and a pair of jeans. He had a white beard and was very friendly with me. My first impression (not that you could trust those at the Cecil—or anywhere) was that Peter was a decent guy.

What was strange about Peter and Kia Conroy was that they were sharing a room. I thought it wasn't optimal, but I assumed that Peter was a sweet father who was taking care of his stunted daughter. Maybe she couldn't live by herself for some reason.

Then one day Pedro and I went to inspect the room, and what did we find?

One bed.

The Cecil rooms, as I have reiterated now many times but cannot reiterate enough, were tiny. There was barely enough room for two people, period. But here the Conroys were not only squishing into the same room together, they were also squishing into the same bed?

A quick scan of their room presented more problems. It was not clean—and I mean really not clean. The state of the room violated guidelines. The sheets were balled up on the bed, and it smelled like the rotten food that had been left out, and of course, this had attracted cockroaches, which were crawling in and out of open cans of food. On top of the single dresser were two TVs, each playing a different channel. After I saw that, it was hard not to imagine this father and daughter duo lying in bed, each enjoying their individual programming—even though it must have been hard to hear with the competing noise of the other TV.

I stated the obvious. "You can't have open containers of food in here like this." I told them they needed to clean it up. This was in the very beginning of us doing the inspections, before the fumigator was coming on a monthly basis. Unfortunately, the sight of some cockroaches had become sort of normal by that point, and I was used to the "clean up your food" spiel.

What I didn't say anything about—what I couldn't say anything about, because Kia was over eighteen—was the fact that these family members were sharing a tiny bed in a tiny room. I was aghast, but there was nothing to do about it.

After we left that day, Pedro gave me the lowdown. He told me that Peter had lived at the Cecil for many years on his own. Then one day, a woman (was it her mother?) dropped Kia off. Kia was about seventeen or eighteen years old then. Nobody ever thought Kia was

Peter's girlfriend because she called him "Daddy." Pedro remembered her, younger, walking out of the lobby with her backpack on. He assumed she was going to school.

Or she just liked backpacks. Every time I saw Kia in the lobby, she was carrying a backpack and she was walking quickly, as if she was late for something. She often wore the same outfit: a pair of jeans and a T-shirt without a bra underneath. This was hard to miss because Kia wasn't exactly flat-chested. There were a lot of people who weren't thriving at the Cecil—the vast majority of them, actually—but Kia's youthfulness, her lack of teeth, and her strange bed-sharing situation really bothered me.

Unlike some of the other tenants, the Conroys did succeed at cleaning up their room. When we went back to reinspect, it was cleaner—although it was still by no means "clean" according to regular standards. But for the Cecil, it was good enough.

Financial struggles were also part of this picture. I received many handwritten notes from Kia explaining that the rent was going to be late. I remember feeling so sorry for her and appreciating her handwritten notes. Whenever she informed me the rent was going to be a little late, I let it go. Of course, I never knew what went on in that room. My sense, though, was that the reason these two shared a bed was money-driven, rather than sex-related. I think they were just trying to make do with the little they had.

As the years passed, the only thing that changed dramatically was Peter's heath. At some point, he began to decline rapidly, and it wasn't long before he was in a wheelchair. Then he started leaving in an ambulance a lot. It became a normal sight to see paramedics rolling him by the front desk on a stretcher. Toward the end, he probably never should have been released from the hospital, but, well, he was. Rumor had it that he'd suffered several strokes and could no longer care for himself.

And so his daughter became his caregiver. She was responsible for changing the adult diapers that her father was confined to wearing. Instead of properly disposing of them, she'd leave them outside the door or in the communal bathrooms. I received many valid complaints from the housekeeping staff to the effect of: "This should not be my responsibility." The truth was that the housekeeping staff at the Cecil did a lot that was beyond the call of duty, and beyond the realm of "normal."

During my last year at the Cecil, the Conroys took $18,500 in exchange for relocating, which is what we offered all the tenants at the end as an incentive for them to move. To my knowledge, they moved down the street, into another hotel in the neighborhood that's similar to the Cecil. It's called the Alexandria. This was where a lot of our tenants relocated. Often, when I drive by, I wonder what happened to Kia and Peter Conroy. In my imagination, Peter is most likely dead and Kia is rushing through the lobby with her backpack on, older now, but still somehow young.

Along with our sometimes-irrational tenants, YouTube sleuths kept sneaking in to film their movies, and homeless people kept shooting up and having sex in the alley. And I continued to go to the courthouse, because either I or the hotel was constantly getting sued. Many people might have found these elements too distressing to handle, and maybe my 2007 self would have agreed. By the last several years at the Cecil, though, I could handle a lot. I'd grown sort of immune to the drama and the danger, and that wasn't really the lens through which I saw the hotel anyway.

I saw myself as a caretaker, and I saw the hotel as the place that needed me. I saw it as an atmosphere of compassion and warmth. Contrary to what its exterior might have suggested to other people, the Cecil was where I came to feel safe. Sometimes I wonder if it was the home I'd always wanted as a kid. Unlike the chaos of my childhood, the chaos of the Cecil was tangibly containable. I was in charge. I had control. I guess that, in and of itself, is a form of safety.

CHAPTER 15

Closing

In 2016, Richard Born came up with a new vision for the Cecil. He decided to lease it out. New York–based Simon Baron Development signed a ninety-nine-year ground lease on the hotel with the plan to close the hotel down, renovate the whole building, and reopen it as "all-inclusive" micro apartments. Currently, Simon Baron Development is paying about $3 million a year to lease the Cecil. And Pedro, as I mentioned, still works there.

Right after this sale went through, I was notified that the members of Simon Baron Development would be flying out from New York to discuss next steps. I was nervous. What did "next steps" mean?

They called a big meeting in the conference room, which was the same conference room where Steve and I had worked on our personal laptops years earlier. I sat down and looked at the strangers around me. These people would be managing the future of the hotel. And then one of them told me what the first next step was.

"We're closing," he said.

"Closing?"

Even though the clock had been ticking loud on the Cecil for a while, it was still surreal to hear that it was finally happening. I was told that I would be given a severance payment, and that none of the other employees would be informed of the imminent closing. This was not what I wanted to hear. The ship was going down, but I was going to be the only one who knew about it? I suppose that in a way, it was a kindness not to tell the other employees. What would it do but worry them? In another way, though, I felt like I was lying by not telling them. I did tell Pedro, of course. I needed somebody else to be in on the truth with me, and since Pedro and I had done everything together for so many years, I absolutely couldn't not tell him.

I learned that the hotel would be closing in the summer of 2016, but I didn't start laying anyone off until that November. It was a horrible experience to have to keep the fates of our employees hidden from them for six months, but I think that probably paled in comparison to the day I had to tell them.

On that day, I called a company-wide meeting. I was incredibly anxious and sad. About 80 percent of our staff didn't speak English as a primary language, so Pedro was right by my side, translating. I remember looking out at this little sea of people I'd come to know so well. Even though most of us didn't speak the same language, I felt deeply connected to them. I'd been their boss for years. And now I was going to have to tell them they were about to be out of a job.

I'm sure I started with an apology. "I'm so sorry to have to deliver this news, but the hotel is closing." I told them that their last day would be December 31, 2016, and that if they could continue to work until then, it would be very appreciated. What made this doubly hard was that after I said it, I had to wait for Pedro to translate to get their reactions. Everybody was understandably upset. The day I left the Cecil for the last time was the saddest, and this was the second saddest.

In an effort to give our employees a path forward, I set up a job fair for them. For whatever reason, none of them wanted to take advantage of that. I suppose they formed their own plans. Most of them kept working until the end of 2016, which I was very happy about. I wanted to reward them for that, and I thought it would be great to go out with a bang, so I made the holidays as jovial as possible that last year. It was a melancholy time, but it was also a grateful one. There's something about being on a sinking ship that brings people together.

Many years earlier, back in the era of Steve, Pedro and I had bought a giant fake Christmas tree somewhere in the Arts District for about $500. It was beyond our meager budget and so gargantuan that it seemed almost cartoonlike. From the first year on, Pedro was very strict about when the tree would go up. It could not make an appearance until the day after Thanksgiving, he said, no way. This became a running joke between us.

Every year, I'd say, "Pedro, can we put the tree up early this year?"

And he would say, "No, Price."

That final year, I thought he might cave. "Pedro, it's the *last* time we're going to put it up. Let's do it early!"

"No," he said. "The tree goes up after Thanksgiving."

And so we did just that. It was a beautiful last Christmas. And December 31, we said goodbye to most of our employees. After that, it was just me, Pedro, and a few others. We became super close during those last months as we helped nudge our beloved hotel closer to its end. We started selling off the desks in the offices and other pieces of furniture. Letting these tangible objects go made it all seem more real.

Because Simon Baron Development was based in New York, nobody was there to manage our day-to-day schedules, so it felt like we were on a ghost ship moving through a dense fog.

On March 2, 2017, the Cecil was officially named a historic landmark by the City of Los Angeles. This sounds fancy, and I suppose that it is, but the true purpose of this designation is the attached tax break. On the day that the hotel became an official landmark, a large group of people arrived for a celebratory tour. I sort of expected the new owners to be involved in the tour, but no, it was me. Maybe this speaks to why I felt like a mother at the Cecil. I was taking care of it constantly, as if it were an abandoned child.

I had toured the Cecil so many times by this point that I could have done it blindfolded. "Hi, I'm Amy. I'm the general manager of this hotel." While walking through the lobby, I'd point at the floors and say, "These are original terrazzo floors." I'd point to the ceiling and say, "And that is original stained glass." In a way, giving this particular tour felt similar to when I took Elisa Lam's parents up to the roof. I somehow couldn't believe that I, Amy, had been granted the power to lead in these crucial moments.

A few more months went by. The few of us remaining continued to take care of loose odds and ends. May 2 was my last day at the Cecil. I absolutely knew the day was coming, but it felt too painful to think about. We had all been through so much. Some of the new owners had flown in the day before. At around two o'clock, one of them came into my office and said, "You can go home early."

My stomach immediately tied into knots and started hurting, but

I didn't show them my distress. "Sure," I said, "thanks."

I was then asked for my keys. That part upset me more than I thought it would. I was handing over the keys to what had become my kingdom, my zoo, and my home. As I looked around there wasn't much left to pack up, and I thought about how the tiniest moments in life can become, well, your entire life. I had dedicated the last ten years to a dream that had unfurled on a random night in Hermosa Beach when Cindy said, "Steve has this project downtown . . ." The only reason I'd said yes was because after I got laid off, I had time. I was spending my days collecting sand dollars on the beach. And that was exactly what I planned to do next.

Once I was ready, Pedro walked me out to the parking lot. On my very first day, I had thought the towering hotel looked ominous. And on my last day, what I saw was Pedro standing in its shadow, smiling at me.

CHAPTER 16

Behind the Door

Of all the tenants at the Cecil, the story of the woman behind the door haunts me the most. That is why I've titled this book after her. Behind the door of every room, there were secrets, but what was lurking in room 242 was shocking. Even now, when I think about what happened in this room, I get angry, and sometimes I want to cry. Unsurprisingly, this story begins and ends with Pedro.

In 2009, Stay had been open for a year, and even though I hadn't technically been anointed general manager yet, I was basically in charge, and more in touch with the everyday workings of the hotel than anyone else. As I mentioned earlier, when I arrived at the Cecil in 2007, the place was, to put it bluntly, a mess. Most of the tenants had been incentivized to move down to floors two and three, and the overall vibe of those floors was especially bleak. The hallways were filled with a haze of cigarette smoke and the blaring sounds of the color TVs that were bolted down to the dilapidated dressers in each room. As with all the other public spaces in the hotel, there was a dedicated houseman who was responsible for cleaning the hallways and the shared bathrooms and showers. The rooms themselves, though, were not cleaned by our staff, and some of them hadn't been checked in many years. That was because the previous owners had not made inspections a priority, so most of the tenant room conditions were unknown.

The opening of Stay required figuring out a bunch of new protocols for how we would run the hotel, and many of those protocols were then applied to the Cecil. So far, I've mentioned checking IDs and requiring credit cards. Another new rule we implemented at the Cecil was mandatory room cleanings. To me, this was very exciting. I thought it meant that we had a real chance at making the building a more habitable place. I thought we'd get rid of all the pest infestations once and for all.

In order to get a better idea of how, exactly, we were going to implement our new protocol, I first needed to know who all the tenants were. The Cecil was so big (six hundred rooms) that it was easy to get lost. I'd never met a lot of our tenants.

And thus began my tenant education. Over the course of several days, Pedro and I sat in my office and started going down the list of names on the tenant rent roll. At this point, we still had about eighty tenants, and all of them were listed on an Excel sheet next to their room number, the amount of rent they paid, and the date they'd moved in. Since Pedro had been at the Cecil for so long, the purpose of our conversations was for him to tell me what he knew. I'd read out a name, and he would respond with snippets of information about the person.

When I got to Mr. Channing's name, there was a name next to it that I hadn't seen before. Dal Harrison.

"Who is that?" I asked.

"The woman," Pedro said.

According to Pedro, Mr. Channing had been at the Cecil for a very long time, roughly forty years. This was odd, because according to his file, he and Dal Harrison had moved in in 2004.

Well, Pedro said, 2004 was likely the date that they'd moved from one of the upper floors down to the second floor, though there was no database with the information, just outdated spreadsheets. Like most of the other tenants in the building, Mr. Channing had agreed to relocate to another room within the building. This, as I mentioned before, was part of an effort to designate a specific area of the hotel for tenants so that the rest could be used just for guests.

"Why have I never seen this woman?" I asked. "How long has she been here?"

According to Pedro, she had been brought into the room about ten years after Mr. Channing moved in, so she'd probably been at the Cecil for about thirty years.

"She is an Asian woman," Pedro added. "She went into the room, but she didn't come out."

"When was the last time she was seen?"

"Never," Pedro said.

"*Never*?" I couldn't quite believe what I was hearing. "So you're telling me that in room two forty-two, there is a woman who Mr. Channing brought in thirty years ago and she hasn't been seen since then, not even once?"

"Yes," Pedro confirmed. He told me that in the early days, the woman (whose name may or may not have been Dal Harrison) could be seen walking down the hallway to the shower with just a sheet around her. He had never seen her with any clothes on. She only wore this sheet. Her hair was long, dark, and wild. Maybe it hadn't been cut in a very long time.

Because room 242 had no shower in it, I said, "If she hasn't left the room, then has she stopped showering?"

"Probably," Pedro said.

This is when my head started to spin. It just seemed so unbelievable. When I dove deeper into Mr. Channing's file, there was a lot of missing information. No previous address was listed. And Dal Harrison's birth date was allegedly the same as Mr. Channing's. This seemed even more unbelievable.

Before I continue, let me tell you about Mr. Channing. He was in his late sixties when I arrived at the Cecil, about six feet tall, and he always wore a black hat over his gray hair. He used a cane, and as he walked, he always seemed to be making strange growling noises. His demeanor was unpleasant and unfriendly. He almost never spoke to me, and when he did, I noticed that his voice was very low and very deep—maybe the deepest voice I'd ever heard. He wasn't, to my knowledge, a smoker. But he was a Vietnam vet.

Now back to the story: All the tenants in the building were advised that their rooms would be properly inspected. We gave them enough notice to clean up on their own if they felt compelled to do so. As the day to inspect Mr. Channing's room approached, my suspense grew. I couldn't wait to see what was going on in there.

Finally, the day arrived. Pedro and I went to the door together. I could hear the TV blaring from inside. Pedro knocked, and Mr. Channing, in his deep, gruff voice, answered, "Just a minute."

We waited. And then a moment later, he opened the door just a crack—and the smell almost caused me to fall over. Putrid. Rank. Rancid. I'm not sure any of these words are enough to capture the insane stench of that room. It was like ammonia and rotten eggs caught in a steam room together, which made it very hard to concentrate.

"We're here to inspect the room," I said to Mr. Channing, who was standing there defensively with his cane.

He grunted and then hesitantly opened the door the rest of the way.

Pedro and I walked in. My most vivid memory, beyond the smell, was the temperature. It really was like a steam room, so incredibly hot, and of course this just intensified the smell. At first, I thought the heat was due to the season. It was fall, the hottest time in Los Angeles. On top of that, the rooms at the Cecil were tiny and the circulation was poor. Then I realized that in addition to all these causes of heat, Mr. Channing had a heater running in the room.

What? Why?!

After I'd found my bearings, my eyes went to the bed, which was covered in a mess of white sheets. The outline of a human body was immediately evident.

I looked at Mr. Channing. "Is the person who's hiding under this sheet okay?" I asked.

"Yes," he grunted. "She's okay."

Just then, a cockroach skittered over the sheet, and that's when I realized that cockroaches were running the show in room 242. There were dozens of them. I looked around and saw them everywhere: running up the curtains and over the TV set and down to the floor. I remembered a fact I had learned from our Ecolab contact, who had much more experience than me with cockroaches: if you see them during the day, that's a big problem. The reason for the infestation wasn't hard to find. All over the room, there were half-drunk liters of soda and open containers of food.

Right when I thought the room couldn't get any more disgusting than it already was, I noticed the bucket parked next to the bed. I instinctually knew that it was being used as a toilet, because, as I said before, room 242 had no bathroom.

"Are you sure that whoever is under that sheet is okay?" I asked again, and more loudly this time. I wanted to give the woman a chance to answer.

She didn't answer. She didn't even move. Only the cockroaches did. I wanted so badly to pull the sheet back and see the woman's face, but I couldn't do that. This was where the situation got sticky. Hiding under some sheets in a very dirty room was strange, but it wasn't illegal.

I told Mr. Channing that the conditions of the room were unacceptable and that he needed to clean it. In addition to that, I informed him that we would be sending a fumigator to address the roach infestation, and that everyone would have to vacate the room for an allotted time period because of the toxins in the formula. Mr. Channing grunted unhappily. And then we left.

Back in my office, Pedro told me a detail that he'd forgotten to mention earlier. Shortly after the woman had arrived, the hotel had received a phone call from a man who lived somewhere in Asia. Was it China? Thailand? Vietnam? He couldn't remember. The man claimed that his mother had been taken to the hotel and was being held hostage. I asked Pedro if any action had been taken after this call and he said no, it had been ignored.

Was the woman under the sheets the mother of the man who had called from Asia? If so, how had he known she was there? Had she snuck out in her early days at the hotel to place a phone call? There were telephones in every room. Maybe she'd called her son collect? Could that have been possible? There was another report from Pedro that a person actually came to the hotel in person looking for the same "missing woman" and nothing was done with that visit, either.

I didn't know the answers to any of these questions, but I did know after the inspection of room 242 that something was terribly wrong, and that maybe it was my job to help. What if the woman wanted to leave but felt she couldn't? Who was going to assist her if not me?

The first thing I did was call Steve and tell him what I'd seen. I had naïvely assumed that if I reported the information, something would be done about it. Surely, everyone would be as upset about this woman hidden in room 242 as I was.

Unfortunately, this was not the case. Steve, a questionable person himself (although I didn't know the extent of his immorality back in 2009), essentially told me to let it go. I was stunned. And confused.

"We're not going to do anything?" I asked him. "Are you serious?"

"Do you really want CNN helicopters flying overhead?" he said. "That will give us bad press."

I didn't think bad press mattered in comparison to human suffering, but the horrible truth was that if the woman wasn't asking for help, it wasn't going to be that easy to help her.

We sent our fumigator, Juan, to the room after our first visit. When he arrived, Mr. Channing was there, and so was the woman. This meant that Juan couldn't spray. But they refused to leave. So instead of spraying, Juan applied roach-killing gel to the baseboards around the room.

During this visit, it was clear that Mr. Channing had made no effort to clean up the room, so I reiterated my request that he do so. After that, there wasn't much more to say. So I set the horror of room 242 to the side to deal with other emergencies, but I continued to think about it all the time. The truth was, though, with Steve telling me there was nothing we could do, there genuinely wasn't a lot of headway to be made. Steve was my boss.

In 2010, I was promoted, officially, to general manager of the hotel, and Steve had begun working off-site at his office in Pershing Square. That's when I began to take my efforts to help the woman in room 242 more seriously. How could I get her out of there?

Mr. Channing was a man of routine. He had the same schedule every single day. He left around the same time and returned around the same time with a bag of food. Because the length of his daily absence was so predictable, I thought it would give me the perfect chance to go up and hopefully get the woman out of the room.

The first thing I had to consider, though, was that if the woman had wanted to, she could have left the room on her own. Mr. Channing couldn't have locked her inside. That was impossible. I started to wonder if Stockholm syndrome could be a possibility. Maybe, after spending so long with Mr. Channing, she had fallen in love with him. Was it possible that a person with Stockholm syndrome could be in love with their captor?

I Googled it: "Is Stockholm syndrome real love?"

Stockholm syndrome is a psychological condition that occurs when a victim of abuse identifies and attaches, or bonds, positively with their abuser. This syndrome was originally observed when hostages who were kidnapped not only bonded with their kidnappers, but also fell in love with them.

Well, that answered my question—I mean, sort of. I supposed that the internet probably wasn't going to be able to define "real" love, since love is so subjective, but I did walk away from this search thinking that yes, the woman in 242 probably was suffering from Stockholm syndrome. She had likely lost touch with reality. The only person she had seen for thirty years was Mr. Channing. And just that fact would give anyone a skewed perception. Plus, maybe there were other factors. Did the woman speak English, for example? Was she mentally stable? Why hadn't she spoken when I had entered the room? Also, what did she look like?

One day, after Mr. Channing left, I called the room. There was no answer. I called again. Still no answer. I went up to the room and knocked on the door. No response. The next day, I did the same thing, and the day after that. But I made no progress. I didn't get it. There was no logical reason for this woman not to answer the phone or open the door, and yet that's what she was doing. I didn't give up hope, though. Maybe one day, the woman would tune in to a new way of thinking—one that was driven by logic.

That didn't happen.

Meanwhile, the monthly inspections of room 242 continued, and Mr. Channing continued to fail them. Every time I returned, there were the open food containers and the roaches again. Not only did Mr. Channing refuse to clean the room, he also removed the roach-killing gel that Juan applied to the perimeter. Every month, it was gone. The fumigator was equally perplexed by the woman and the removal of the gel.

Not knowing exactly what to do next, I made a list of organizations that might be able to help. I called the health department, Adult Protective Services, the fire department, and the police department.

The health department turned out to be the most helpful. I reported Mr. Channing for refusing to clean up his room, despite my many requests. And so an official from the health department agreed to come and check it out.

When Mr. Channing opened the door and saw the official there, he looked so angry. The official immediately recognized that there was a problem. Living in these conditions was not okay. He wrote Mr. Channing a fix-it ticket.

Did this change anything?

No.

What happened next was a curveball.

Mr. Channing added a dog to the mix.

Were pets allowed at the Cecil?

No, they definitely were not. And the dog that Mr. Channing brought in (or found?) was not trained. It was a vicious, unwashed thirty-pound animal that seemed feral. It barked all the time. I often could hear the barking while I was in my office. After all, he was only one floor above me. I believe that I saw the dog on the day it arrived at the hotel. Mr. Channing tied a rope around its neck instead of a leash, and as he walked by the front desk, I said, "Dogs are not allowed here."

He ignored me and kept walking.

I responded by sending Mr. Channing a notification reminding him that dogs were not allowed in the building. The next day, he presented me with documentation that alleged his new pet was an emotional support animal. The letter stated that Mr. Channing had no close relatives to help him with his conditions. I thought, *No close relatives? What about the woman in the bed, who Mr. Channing alternately referred to as his wife or his sister?*

After the dog arrived, it was the three of them—Mr. Channing, the woman, and the dog—suffering in the hot, hot room. Mr. Channing continued to refuse to clean, and he continued to remove the gel whenever Juan applied it. The health department arrived again and gave him another ticket, which did nothing.

One important thing to note is that because we were legally required to give Mr. Channing advance notice that we would be inspecting his room, he had time to make changes. No, he never cleaned the room, but every time we went in there, the bucket by the bed was empty. If it had been full, the health department would have absolutely had a more severe response than a fix-it ticket, and Mr. Channing likely knew this.

Time went on. At some point, we had to repipe the building. This meant that one of our maintenance workers, a guy named Johnny, needed to enter room 242 to do some caulking. Here is the statement that Johnny gave after his visit to the room:

Friday, January 10th at 10:30am, Johnny entered Mr. Channing's room to conduct some caulking to the pipe in his unit. Mr. Channing answered after Johnny knocked on the door. As he entered the room, a powerful and intoxicating smell of feces and urine hit his nose at once. The pipe Johnny had to work on was located behind the dresser, across the room, allowing him to view the condition of the entire room. Mr. Channing was accompanied by his wife and their service pet dog in this room. His wife lay on the bed, covering herself from head to toe to avoid being seen. The bed was filled with cockroaches that crawled all over her body. The dog appeared to be malnourished. There was a bucket by the sink that looked like it contained human waste along with additional feces and urine all over the floor in the unit. The condition of this unit was very disturbing and appeared uninhabitable. Please see the attached diagram drawn by Johnny for details.

Mr. Channing had forgotten to empty the waste bucket before Johnny entered. This was the only time a third party saw the bucket being used for waste. When I called the health department to report this, there was, again, not much they could do. Unless one of their officials actually saw the waste, then it couldn't be considered a fact.

As more time passed, I kept feeling like I had to do something, but I didn't know what to do. When I thought of the mysterious woman, I felt so upset. And it was the same with the dog. The fact that living creatures were being abused under my watch was unbearable.

I called Animal Protective Services about the dog. When they arrived to inspect the situation, they asked Mr. Channing if he ever took the dog on walks. I don't remember what he said, but I do know that the dog, like the woman, never emerged from the room after it went in. Which meant that both of them were sharing the bucket.

On the day Animal Protective Services came, Mr. Channing tied the rope around the dog's neck and took it for a walk. It might have been the only walk that dog took while Mr. Channing was its owner.

Later on, the dog exited the picture. To be honest, I don't quite remember what happened to it, but I was glad that it was gone. I hoped it had landed somewhere better.

Then the plot thickened again.

Not long after Animal Protective Services came, I received a call informing me that Mr. Channing wanted to see me in the lobby. When I went to greet him, he handed me a stack of papers and said in his gruff voice, "You've been served. See you in court."

Technically, you're not supposed to serve the person you're suing yourself, but obviously Mr. Channing didn't care about rules.

"Served for what?" I said.

"Read it," Mr. Channing growled, then walked toward the elevator bank.

Surprised, I took the papers back to my office and looked at them.

"What the fuck? A restraining order? Me?"

I literally said this out loud to myself. I was beyond shocked. And it all just seemed so unfair. How could a man who was keeping a woman hostage in a roach-infested room be serving me with a restraining order?

Mr. Channing claimed that I was harassing him by coming to his room all the time, and that I'd harassed him about his emotional service animal.

Reading through the papers, I didn't understand why Dal Harrison was referred to by a new name. Dalia Harry. It was so strange. Had he forgotten his other pseudonym for her? Or was that intentional?

Another interesting detail was that Mr. Channing had typed up his complaint. Where had he gone to do that? He didn't have a computer. Had somebody helped him? I'd always wondered where he went all day long, since I knew he didn't work. Since he was a vet, I assumed he was on some type of government assistance.

Pedro took me to court on the day our case was tried. Often, Pedro would drive me in my car to the familiar courthouse on Hill

Street. I was usually attending the case solo, although sometimes I'd go with a lawyer. Pedro would always say, "Good luck, Price. Call me when you are finished."

When our case was called, Mr. Channing walked with his limp and cane to the wrong side of the courtroom. Nobody corrected him. What I seemed to be learning over and over was that rules could be broken without punishment—and that people who followed all the rules were sometimes punished anyway for no good reason.

Mr. Channing and I approached the judge, who looked at us both intently, probably wondering what the real story was.

"So, I understand, Mr. Channing, that you would like a restraining order against Miss Price," the judge said.

There was a long pause. And then Mr. Channing answered, "No, no. Ugh, I don't want a restraining order against Miss Price. Not her. I want a restraining order against the security guard who's posting notices on my door. They're always trying to inspect my room."

Of course, I was the one who requested that the notices be posted on his door, which Mr. Channing either did or did not know. From a technical angle, it was confusing that he'd served me if the person he'd really intended to sue was the security guard.

"If the restraining order is not meant for Miss Price, then you need to refile it," the judge said.

And then he closed the case and told us to go home.

Mr. Channing never filed another restraining order against me. I never got him to clean his room, and I was unable to get the health department to do anything to help the woman hiding underneath the sheets. I did convince Adult Protective Services to come investigate after calling them numerous times. Nobody answered the door when they came, and they didn't try again. I also requested that the fire department come help the woman. They came, took her vitals, said she was doing fine, and left. I felt like I was going crazy. How could everybody else be letting this happen? How had I tried in so many ways to help this woman and gotten nowhere?

Mr. Channing and I were at a standstill.

And it would remain like that for years.

Then, when the ownership changed again (I'll explain this in more detail later) I was given a new chance to try to help the woman behind the door. The new owners started a relocation incentive program in an effort to implore tenants to leave the building. A social worker met with each of the tenants individually to help decide what was best for them. If the tenant left, they were offered compensation. When this process began, I informed the new owners and the social workers of what I had seen in room 242.

The social workers met with Mr. Channing and the woman together in their room. This was the very first time I saw her face. She looked . . . too happy, which suggested to me that she probably wasn't mentally well. And her hair—it was so long, and piled on top of her head like Marge Simpson's, but not styled, more like it hadn't been washed or combed for a long time. Next to her were a roll of toilet paper and box of Cheese Nips. Later, I would learn that she had very few teeth, and I imagined her putting the crackers in her mouth (or maybe Mr. Channing did it) and letting them slowly dissolve.

During the meeting, she did not speak. Mr. Channing explained that he wanted to receive the compensation for a relocation, but he was told that in order to do that, the woman underneath the sheets would need to produce a valid ID. This was their way of trying to get her into a more humane situation. "Let's get her an ID," they said, "and maybe a haircut, too."

Mr. Channing claimed that the woman (who he referred to as his wife in the interactions with Adult Protective Services) had lost her ID many years earlier. Multiple times, over the course of the next few weeks, the social workers tried to secure a date on which they'd take the woman to get a haircut and some fresh clothes. Every appointment was either canceled or they simply didn't show up. Eventually, Mr. Channing dropped the dream of relocation.

Two years later, in 2017, after I had left my job at the Cecil, Pedro and a houseman named Julio were walking past room 242 and detected the familiar scent of death. When they opened the door, they found Mr. Channing dead in his bed.

Next to him was the woman, alive and well and smiling.

The paramedics removed Mr. Channing's body. They put the woman on a stretcher and took her away.

Pedro called me right after it happened and yelled, "He's dead! Mr. Channing died."

"What happened to the woman?" I asked.

"They took her away," Pedro said.

Pedro went on to say that as the woman was being wheeled out of the lobby on a stretcher, she was laughing out loud. Pedro mimicked how that sounded. "She kept doing a 'HA HA HA' as she was being taken away for medical support." That really shook me. The fact that she was cackling away after being in that atrocious situation for way too many years and found lying next to the creep's dead body.

Nobody ever came to collect Mr. Channing's belongings. Unsurprisingly, nobody ever came to inquire about the woman, either. I am still in disbelief that there was never a follow-up. What happened to this woman? Where is she now?

Pedro and Julio cleaned up room 242, and now it is vacant.

Did I do enough? What more could I have done? When I think of the woman now, these are the questions that still haunt me. It never felt right, and it still doesn't. Pedro has encouraged me to try to get to the bottom of it, but like a lot of other things, it was never resolved.

CHAPTER 17

Other Tenants I Still Think About

The woman behind the door was, to me, the Cecil's most memorable tenant, but I want to tell you about a few others as well. There was a woman named Lauren Sanford, for instance, who made an everlasting impression on me.

Lauren was a wild-looking woman. She was in her midfifties, maybe five foot four, and she wore fake eyelashes long before they were popular. This detail is extra memorable to me because of how imperfect Lauren's lashes were. She often had a full set glued to one eyelid, and on the other eyelid, only a few scragglers remained. The glue strip always seemed to be about to fall off her eyelid, and she put her mascara on thickly and lazily, which caused a lot of clumps.

Adding to her asymmetrical look was a wig that wasn't hanging evenly a lot of the time. I think it's safe to say that Lauren was not the best stylist. Her foundation was always the wrong color, and it appeared to have been applied over a layer of Vaseline. I once overheard her telling another tenant that she did her makeup in the shower. I wasn't sure if this was true or not. It did seem like the type of unique thing Lauren would do, but then again, she lied all the time.

Another marked characteristic of Lauren's was her volume. Lauren was loud. When she was coming, you were aware of it.

"Amy Price!"

She liked to use my whole name when she addressed me, which she did often. She'd come down to the lobby demanding to speak with me. Sometimes she was in a huff, which just made her louder. Usually, when she appeared, she would be wearing a tattered terry cloth robe, furry bedroom slippers, and a green cold cream mask covering her face. The only parts of her face that weren't green were her eyes and those unforgettable eyelashes.

Lauren moved in as a student in 2008. That year, we were scrambling for income at the Cecil, so we offered reduced rates for students. (This is different from what we would offer at Stay about a year later.) Lauren established her residency at the Cecil as a full-time student of Los Angeles Community College. I still have her class schedule, which she presented as proof of her scholarly efforts. She was taking classes in law and management. I don't know who let Lauren move in—who thought she would be a good tenant?—but it definitely wasn't me.

Lauren lived in room 819, which I will never forget, because when she wasn't demanding to speak with me in the lobby, she was leaving me angry voice mails in which she always identified herself by her room number.

"Amy Price, it's Lauren Sanford, room eight nineteen."

Lauren was a problem from the moment she walked into the

building. Even in the beginning, she struggled to pay her rent. She was served many three-day notices as a result. She was not the type to say, *I'm sorry, I'm late on the rent.* Her style was to say something along the lines of, *Fuck you! I'll pay when I want!*

Shortly after Lauren arrived at the Cecil, she added a boyfriend to the mix, which was another problem. Sometimes she would call the front desk when she was in the middle of a violent argument with her boyfriend and scream at me that he needed to be removed from the property immediately. The police would be called as a result. And then a few weeks later, the same thing would happen again.

Lauren never seemed to react to anything logically. It was impossible to predict what she would do next. Sometimes this was merely annoying. Other times, it was scary. I'm positive that Lauren hated my guts, but I'm not sure that it was personal. She might have been angry at everyone.

One evening, Lauren approached me at the front desk and just started yelling "Fuck you!" over and over.

"Fuck you, Amy Price! Fuck you!"

I tried to ignore her and keep doing whatever I'd been doing before her entry. I had found that sometimes, with her, it was best not to add fuel to the fire.

Well, my plan totally failed.

Before I knew it, Lauren was chucking a glass Coke bottle at my head and screaming, "Amy Price, you white lily-ass bitch!" She then repeated the word "bitch" for what seemed like an entire minute.

The glass bottle missed my head, thankfully, and hit the mailboxes behind me. This moment was even more petrifying for me than when one of our tenants, Sam, chased me down the street screaming, "I'm gonna get you!"

Needing to gather my wits, I went up to my office, where I noticed that my heart was pounding much faster than usual. My fear eventually subsided, and then I moved on. That's how I always dealt with the madness at the Cecil. I took a deep breath and then I moved on.

I wish that were the end of the Lauren story, but it's not. Along with throwing a bottle at my head and incessantly harassing me over the course of multiple years, Lauren, like some of the other of the Cecil's most memorable tenants, loved to complain.

Sometimes she would call the health department to report us. This ended up backfiring every time because Lauren was a hoarder. The health department official would arrive, inspect her room, and give her a citation. One inspector referred to her space as a fire hazard and after a visit wrote, "Advised occupant to decrease the materials and personal belongings inside the room." They also observed "a lack of elbow room," which is really understating the situation, but I found it to be hilarious.

When Lauren wasn't calling the health department, she was taking us to court. The legal file labeled LAUREN SANFORD was thicker than any other tenant's. We were in court with her constantly.

In 2012, she filed a discrimination lawsuit. Her first claim, in her own words, was this: "Management stated I was not the right kind of person for the hotel. I believe that this statement refers to my race." Her second claim was: "There are no black tenants at Stay hotel."

We hired an expensive lawyer to handle the case, and I'd be lying if I didn't say I was absolutely horrified. What Lauren was accusing me of was so out of line with anything I'd ever say or do. My response to the first allegation was, "At no time has such a statement ever been communicated to Ms. Sanford. It is simply untrue."

My response to the second allegation was, "There are not any tenants at The Stay Hotel. However, when we did have student housing (before April 2011), there were black tenants. The Cecil Hotel (the sister property) currently has 22 black tenants, 13 Hispanic tenants, and 4 white tenants."

As soon as her lawsuit was deemed invalid, she filed another one with similar themes. This kept going and going. It just became status quo to always be in a lawsuit with Lauren.

When we offered Lauren the $18,500 compensation to relocate, interacting with her about the relocation was uncomfortable, because we were embroiled in yet another lawsuit with her at the time. And Lauren was not making the relocation thing easy. Actually, the way she interpreted it made no sense. Her plan was to take the $18,500, but not hand over the keys. When I explained to her that in order to receive the check, she had to leave the property and surrender any future claims to it as a residence, her response was, "Fuck you, Amy Price!"

One day at the courthouse, Lauren's lawyer couldn't locate her. She had just left the building. Another time, her attorney was overheard saying that he couldn't control his client. This was not a surprise. Lauren was absolutely uncontrollable.

In the end, we secured an unlawful detainer, which basically meant that Lauren was evicted from the property. Somehow, though, we still paid her the relocation fee. The fact that Lauren managed to pull that off was as unsurprising as her behavior in court. I think we were all so worn down by her that it seemed easier to pay her off rather than to keep fighting.

To make matters even more unfair, I was forced to write a letter to Lauren's new landlord saying that she'd been a wonderful tenant who paid her rent on time. I should mention here that during my time at the Cecil, I evicted many tenants for not paying their rent, and in most cases, that information was sealed, which is to say that it was not disclosed. The tenant's future landlord would have no way of knowing what problems they were signing up for. Lauren Sanford and many others left with a perfect history. I thought it was so unjust. The fact that Lauren requested a letter and got it is exactly the same as her being paid to be evicted. She was excellent at working the system, mostly because she was just so loud, disruptive, and sometimes dangerous.

In 2013, Lauren filed yet another lawsuit. I don't even remember what it was about. I do remember, though, that it was investigated and then dismissed because of insufficient evidence. After that, our lawyer advised us to file an anti-SLAPP (Strategic Lawsuit Against Public Participation) motion, which prevented Lauren from being able to sue us ever again.

Lauren was merciless in her complaints, and very determined, and neither she nor her makeup made any sense at all. When I think of her now, I imagine her in her terry cloth robe with that green cold cream mask on her face screaming, "Amy Price, fuck you!"

Another tenant who made a big impression was Mike Mayley.

Mike was in his sixties, around five foot five, and he always wore a sleeveless jean jacket with a white tank top underneath, paired with jeans. He was extremely paranoid and reeked of cigarettes. Sometimes Mike would stop at the front desk and tell me details about his life that didn't seem very pertinent. His jean jacket, for example: he got it at the Goodwill. My impression was that Mike was mentally ill.

The combination of Mike's paranoia and his love of chitchat meant that he frequently reported bad behavior he'd witnessed in the building to me. Sometimes the information was helpful. Most of the time, it wasn't, because Mike's brain didn't exactly function in the most rational way. Once he started a joke:

"Why did the chicken cross the road?"

And when I asked why, he walked away. I think that was the end of the joke?

I got the impression that Mike saw me as his friend, and I think he was starved for friends. He didn't appear to have any. Most of the tenants didn't.

The inspection of Mike's room was basically a study in how cigarette smoke wreaks havoc on a building over time. His door frame had turned yellow from the smoke that was constantly wafting its way from his room into the hallway. It wasn't a dirty room, or at least not in the way that most other tenants' rooms were dirty. There were no open food containers or roaches. There was just a layer of nicotine covering every surface. The furniture, the walls, and the ceiling were coated so thickly in cigarette film that you could scrape your fingernail over them and then need to go to the sink immediately to wash it off.

Along with coming up to the front desk and telling me random details about his life, Mike also liked to tell me about the nefarious things other tenants were doing. Here is a note he once left for me:

Amy,

On the evening of June 16th, 2008, at approximately 6:37 or 7:31 on the video cameras, you can see Simon selling codeine to two Mexican men at the entrance of the hotel. Also, the African American in room 303 still smokes crack. I smelled it early Sunday morning. And the pregnant woman in 305 was yelling at other guests.

Mike had a particularly hard time with one tenant, Darren Lawrence, otherwise known as DJ. Mike was afraid of DJ, because allegedly DJ was harassing him. Here is a note he left me about that:

I am sick with the flu. Why did the security guard, whatever his name is, bang his fist in my door eight times very loudly? I don't need this harassment. Also, I was walking down the hall by room 318. I walked by a shower next to 318 and DJ swung the door open and said, "Look, Mike, I'm wearing a towel!" He was badgering me like he has many times before, as I told you.

DJ always seemed so normal to me, which was why it was hard to take Mike's harassment allegations seriously. DJ, though, as you will see shortly, was suffering, too.

During the relocation period, when we offered Mike the option to leave in exchange for a check, he became even more paranoid. Why were we asking him to relocate? What did we really want? In the end, Mike never made the choice about whether or not to relocate, because he ended up in the hospital. I was never exactly sure why, but my guess was lung cancer or some other smoking-related ailment. He called me from the hospital telling me he had quit smoking. Again, this made me feel like he considered me to be his friend.

While I formed bonds with many of the tenants of the Cecil, some remained mysterious to me. Tarantino Falito was one of those tenants.

He was in his fifties, possibly Hispanic, and very thin. He often wore jeans and a white T-shirt, and on his chin was a slight beard. When he passed by me at the front desk, he was mostly noncommunicative. I thought of him as a quiet, wiry, mysterious man who seemed a little bit off, although I wasn't sure why.

Tarantino first came to my attention at Stay when he started lying down in front of guests' doors and praying in a foreign language—or possibly an invented language; it wasn't clear. Tarantino was a good example of why the shared elevators were a problem. Cecil tenants could very easily gain access to Stay. Tarantino's hallway prayers were reported multiple times. I don't remember exactly what disciplinary action was taken, but I do know that whatever it was inspired him to stop being disruptive in this way.

Many years went by without any disturbance, and then Tarantino became a problem again, but for a very different reason. He lived on the second floor, which is located about twenty feet above the sub-roof, and one day, he stopped using the elevators or the stairs. Instead, he started taking the exterior fire escape up to the sub-roof (which was a restricted area), and from there, he somehow scaled the building to get up to his room. I'm still not sure how he managed this. All I know is that we received multiple reports about a man who appeared to be entering and exiting his room from outside, like Spider-Man.

We asked him to stop. He didn't. And so we proceeded with an eviction case against him. This was the warning notice he was sent:

> You have created a nuisance by exiting your upper floor and walking onto the ledge of the building and up and down fire escapes, despite there being no emergency. You have been given prior notice that the fire escapes are meant to be used as evacuation routes during emergency. Your activity is dangerous to your-

self, and other persons below should you happen to fall or drop
any materials that you may bring outside the building with you.
Due to prior warnings and the fact that you have ignored them,
this is now a non-curable reach. You must vacate your room, or
unlawful detainer action may be filed against you.

The courthouse on Hill Street was one of my most frequented
off-campus haunts while working at the Cecil. That's where I went
every time we were attempting to evict a tenant, and Tarantino's
case was no different. During our hearing, it was revealed that
Tarantino's attorney could not communicate with him because he
was speaking a language that nobody could understand. There were
Spanish-speaking translators readily available in the courthouse,
but they were of no help because clearly, Tarantino was not speaking Spanish. Neither his attorney nor the judge could figure out
what language he was speaking. Eventually, the judge deemed the
language "unidentifiable," and we ended up winning the case. I
had successfully evicted Spider-Man for scaling the exterior of the
building to enter his room.

On the day of the eviction, since he did not leave on his own,
police stepped in to help us remove him. They knocked on his door.
He responded from the other side in his unidentifiable language. He
did not open the door. I was standing in the hall with Pedro, watching and listening to this unfold.

"Do you have a crowbar?" one of the cops asked.

We found them a crowbar, and once they'd gained access to the
room (which had almost nothing in it beyond a few books), they
told Tarantino he had ten minutes to pack up. Shortly after that, he

emerged in a pair of white Fruit of the Loom briefs. He walked out of the hotel like that, in just his underwear. I never saw him again.

What was and wasn't true about our tenants and their pasts was not always clear to me. As I've mentioned, I was often surprised to find out that a tenant I considered to be an upstanding citizen turned out not to be one. Then there were other tenants who I continue to wonder about. Shelly Blanford is one of those.

Shelly was in her fifties. She appeared to be very put together. She wore business-casual clothes and had a job. Allegedly, she worked for a nonprofit called Gift of Life, which fulfilled the dreams of sick children. I thought that was impressive. Why, if she had this great job, was she living at the Cecil? And why was she always a little late on her rent? She had a good excuse every time, and I think I believed her because of her appearance and her alleged job.

That's probably also why I agreed to have a coffee with her. I never did this with tenants, but I made an exception for Shelly. As we drank our coffee, she told me that the Cecil, which she referred to with feminine pronouns, wanted me to write a book.

"She wants you to write a book about her."

Shelly went on to say that she would be happy to assist me with writing the book and that she had experience. "I wrote a book, too," she said.

Was that true? Was it not? Did Shelly really work at Gift of Life?

Like so many of the things that were said at the Cecil, I would never know.

Right now, as I write this book, I am thinking about Shelly telling me that I need to honor the Cecil by sharing some of her stories. Whether or not she wrote a book or worked at Gift of Life seems secondary to the hope she gave me.

Another memorable tenant is a guy named Mr. Tom Cecil.

The funny thing about him is that he dressed like he was the head librarian of an important library. He wore brown trousers with a belt and a dress shirt, and old-fashioned wire-rimmed glasses. He was bald, possibly in his late sixties or early seventies, and pleasant. He wasn't a drug user or a drinker. Even though he was dressed like a head librarian, he didn't have a job. Mr. Cecil was a peculiar man, but for many years, he kept it together. He paid his rent on time. He caused no disturbances. He kept to himself. I'm not sure if he had any friends or family.

Of course, because Tom's last name was Cecil, there were rumors going around that he had a stake in the ownership of the hotel. This is something I never was able to understand. How could anyone think that one of our tenants had a stake in ownership? I highly doubt that anyone with a lot of money would have chosen to live at the Cecil— well, except for Simon Bailey, maybe.

More than once, when Mr. Cecil passed by, I would hear a tenant say something like, "I heard he owns the place."

Besides being hilariously misunderstood, there was nothing out of the ordinary with Mr. Cecil—until he stopped paying his rent. Shortly after this came to my attention, I approached him in the lobby and said, "Mr. Cecil, you haven't paid your rent."

And then he did something that I considered to be very out of character. He looked directly at me and said, "Yes, I haven't paid and I don't plan to pay anymore."

I was taken aback. What had happened to the pleasant, librarian-esque man I knew?

"Mr. Cecil," I said, "you can't not pay your rent. If you want to stay here, then you have to pay."

He repeated his plan. "I'm not paying," he said.

"Okay," I said, "but if you keep not paying, that's going to result in an eviction."

Mr. Cecil laughed in an eerie way and left.

Not long after that, the inevitable happened. He got evicted.

On eviction day, when the police officers knocked on the door, Mr. Cecil was sleeping. It was early, around eight thirty a.m., and because he'd failed to open the door, we had entered the room. He was wearing a V-neck and a pair of boxer shorts. This stuck out to me because I'd only ever seen him in his librarian garb.

"Mr. Tom Cecil?" one of the officers said loudly.

Mr. Cecil woke up then, and propped his head up on a hand.

"You have ten minutes to get changed and leave," the officer said.

Mr. Cecil opted not to change into his usual outfit that day. After he was escorted out of the room, I went inside and saw that outfit hanging in the closet: the brown trousers, the dress shirt, the belt.

Other than that, there was not a single personal item in the room.

In the months that followed, Pedro and I would see Mr. Cecil outside, pointing up at the Cecil and cackling.

"Ha ha ha!"

He didn't look as put together anymore, certainly not like a librarian. Mr. Cecil's story is yet another example of how sometimes, the way in which people suffer is in the form of a quiet progression that gets louder, by surprise, over time.

The story of another tenant, Zach Orzo, is a good example of how working at the Cecil made me more compassionate than I had been before I took the job.

Zach was a short, heavy man in his sixties who wore nice

enough clothes. He was a loner, neither overly friendly nor overly hostile. Spanish was his primary language, but he was able to speak and write in English. His face always looked tired. Over the years, Mr. Orzo left me many notes in which he referred to himself as "The Bohemian."

I first became aware of Mr. Orzo, aka The Bohemian, while we were doing inspections. He was a hoarder, particularly obsessed with collecting newspapers. There was no room to sit down in his room, not even on the bed. As with all the other tenants in the building who were living in conditions that were deemed uninhabitable, I started by requesting that Mr. Orzo fix the problem himself.

Well, Mr. Orzo was unwilling to do that—or at least that's how I saw it at the time. The health department came. More requests were made that Mr. Orzo clean up. He continued to not clean up. I pleaded with Mr. Orzo. I even offered to send up some of our housemen to help him get rid of some stuff. He said no. I tried to support him by creating timelines. I'd tell him he had two weeks left, and then a week, and so on. This did not make a difference.

Eventually, Mr. Orzo, who had been living at the Cecil since 1985, was evicted. By the time that happened, I understood that the problem wasn't unwillingness. It was ability. Mr. Orzo was not capable of making a change to his circumstances, because he was not well. Anybody who is hoarding is not well. That is how I see it now. Hoarding is a symptom of a larger issue.

Working at the Cecil gave me compassion for types of people I might have judged before. Now, whenever anybody mentions a hoarder, the first thing I think is, *It's not their fault.*

When I think of DJ, I am still haunted.

DJ Lawrence was a real piece of work. He was about six foot two, with blond hair, and he always wore a pair of Levi's with a wrinkled white T-shirt and a jean jacket. Literally, he was always in the same outfit. Wearing repeat outfits at the Cecil was a popular thing to do, I'm realizing as I write this. DJ was not dirty or smelly like some of the other tenants, nor did he seem to be mentally unstable—at first.

Yes, in the beginning, DJ seemed very normal. He told me he was a janitor on the Paramount lot. Actually, he worked on some of the same shows that my mom watched on TV every week. At some point, he'd give a signed photograph of a celebrity to me to give to my mother. It was an actor from *CSI* who even bothered to write my mom's name on the photo. I thought that was very generous.

Once, I saw DJ at a bus stop on Melrose on my way to work. My guess was that he was on his way home from work, and I considered pulling over and offering him a ride, but at the last minute, I decided against it. Even though we had a very friendly repartee, I didn't want to set the precedent that I would be driving him home from work regularly. I did mention this to him later, though. "I saw you at the bus stop," I said.

"You should have picked me up!"

I laughed. "I know."

Later, I would think, *Thank god I didn't pick him up.*

DJ was one of the tenants I interacted with the most. He was just in the lobby all the time, and he liked to chat. We were around the same age, which probably made me feel even closer to him. In my mind, he was the Cecil's most stable tenant. He could hold a conversation that made sense while looking you in the eye.

But if he was so stable, then why did he live at the Cecil? I asked myself this question and decided that the answer was probably that he'd meant for the hotel to be a temporary solution to a housing problem. And then, I don't know, maybe the cheap rent kept him there.

I don't remember when I heard the rumors that DJ liked to smoke crack and hire hookers, and that information certainly didn't seem to jibe with the friendly janitor I knew who worked on the Paramount lot and who'd given my mother a signed celebrity photograph.

Every day when he got home from work, at around four p.m., DJ would come up to the front desk and chat with me. For a while, when the gallery was still open, I'd bring my dogs to work and let them run around in there during the day. DJ loved my dogs, and often, during our late-afternoon conversations, he would tell me how cute they were. When I decided to stop bringing the dogs to work, because there were just too many dodgy characters around, DJ was bummed about it.

Now, back to the rumors. You might recall me mentioning earlier that according to Mike Mayley, DJ was obsessed with him and harassing him on a regular basis. This was hard for me to understand, because again, DJ just seemed so stable and nice. It was confusing trying to reconcile the way DJ allegedly behaved toward Mike with the way he behaved toward me.

Just the way he greeted me was so friendly. "Hey, Amy!" he'd say with a smile.

Then one night, neighbors reported a man who fit DJ's description sitting outside on the third-floor fire escape at night, masturbating.

I addressed the issue head-on. When he came home the next

day, I said, "DJ, I've gotten reports about you being out on the fire escape late at night. As you know, those areas are restricted unless it's an emergency."

DJ nodded and smiled in a way that suggested he had possibly not absorbed what I'd just said.

Uncomfortably, I continued, "I've received reports about you doing inappropriate things on the fire escape, which is also not allowed."

After I said that, everything changed.

First, it was his demeanor. He became shifty. Instead of stopping at the front desk to chat, he hurried by, refusing to make eye contact with me. Instead of always coming in around four p.m., he entered and exited the building at random. Had he lost his job? Was that also why he became less dependable with his rent?

This behavior went on for quite a while. Meanwhile, his appearance changed drastically. He probably lost fifty pounds. He continued to wear the same outfit, which fit loosely after a while. He stopped doing his hair. He just looked disheveled.

Then the suicide of the young man whose body I heard land on the roof above my office happened. DJ was the one who reported it. After that, his behavior became even more sketchy. I noticed that he was often sweating profusely. On the rare occasions that I spoke with him, I could see the sweat beads all over his face. One day, he told me that both his parents were dying. It was a heavy conversation—although I'm not sure if they were really dying.

When I left in 2017, DJ was still there. Pedro told me that he'd stopped paying rent and eventually, he'd been evicted. Did he fall into a crack addiction? Or was he unable to pay his rent for other reasons? Was his shame around me finding out about his fire escape escapades part of what led to his downfall? Or would that have happened anyway?

As with all of the other tenants who could still be alive, I wonder where he is now.

CHAPTER 18

Saying Goodbye

What do you do after you've been in charge of a place like the Cecil for a decade?

When I walked out of the hotel in 2017, I was unsure about what the next step would be. The full experience was a lot to wrap my head around. It really did feel like I had lost a family and a kingdom. Even though it was a very dysfunctional family, I still missed them. It was bizarre at first, not getting up in the morning and driving downtown and seeing all the usual characters. It was strange, too, that nobody was calling me from the familiar phone number, telling me about yet another emergency.

The easiest thing for me to do was to put my emotions aside and get back to work, so that's exactly what I did. My first job was for Clive's brother-in-law, who I'd known for years. He hired me to redesign a two-hundred-unit apartment complex near Culver City. I oversaw the entire project and managed it all without drama. This job was easy compared to what I had endured at the hotel. I also redesigned a rehab that Clive had purchased. It consisted of two large houses in Valley Village. Clive was an intelligent guy, and his main drive was making money. And rehabs make a lot of money. The original conditions of the structure were grisly, and I completely revamped them. I considered who would be walking into that rehab and how low they'd probably be feeling when they arrived. Rehab isn't exactly where young children dream about ending up. I chose bright colors and hung signs that said inspirational things, hoping to create an uplifting atmosphere.

The larger projects, like the big apartment complex, increased my confidence as an interior designer and gave me the courage to strike out on my own. I got my own clients. Some of them were celebrities. Before I knew it, I was working independently, and I was making even more money than I had at the hotel.

I felt elated doing these design gigs. It's the same way I feel when I make jewelry. I possess a natural talent for creating beautiful things, and have ever since I was a little kid in Michigan painting snail shells and trying to sell them.

As time passed, I still wasn't sure how, exactly, to define my role at the Cecil. To be honest, I still don't think words can express what it meant to me. And it was confusing, too. I loved it. I hated it. I needed it. It needed me.

Even after I left, I didn't really leave. I was still thinking about the Cecil all the time, and about Pedro and Julio, still there, making sure the building was okay. Pedro started FaceTiming me frequently, and even though that is definitely not my preferred method of communication, I picked up because he's so entertaining.

"What are you doing Friday, Price?" he'd ask me, and before I knew it I was driving back to the Cecil about once a week to have lunch with my old friend. I'd park in my old spot in the parking lot, and then Pedro would come get me and take me into my old office and say, "Sit in your chair."

"It's not my chair anymore, Pedro," I would say.

"Sit in your chair, Price."

I felt melancholy sitting in my old chair, and I wouldn't have done it if Pedro hadn't asked me to.

I know he was sad without me there, and I was sad not to be seeing him every day anymore, too. For ten years, we'd been like two peas in a pod, or like Frick and Frack. I tried to go to the Cecil as often as I could in the months after I left. Pedro and I went to our usual haunts for lunch. Over the years, we'd developed similar tastes, and we had a group of favorite restaurants downtown. The people there know us as good friends. It is easy to see how close we are when we are together. We always laugh and poke each other and smile. I hope that never ends.

Life continued to hum along. I continued doing interior design and selling my jewelry at large trade shows. Retailers would buy from me at wholesale prices and sell the pieces in boutiques. I kept going to hang out with Pedro whenever I could. When people, particularly my design clients, asked about my work experience, I'd tell them I had a history in the hotel world. If they wanted to know more, I'd mention the Cecil. Some people knew that it was a rough place, but nobody in 2017 knew it as the place where the girl had died in the water tank. That wouldn't become its tagline until 2021, when the Netflix docuseries aired.

It was almost exactly a year after leaving the Cecil that I received a phone call that would alter my life.

Who was on the other end of the line?

Teddy, the drug rehab boyfriend I'd met when I was fifteen years old, the one who I'd always considered to be my one true love, and who had spent the majority of his adult years behind bars.

"Amy," he said, "I just got out of prison."

CHAPTER 19

Teddy

I was in Michigan when Teddy called me, which might have made the call seem even more significant. Michigan was where we were both from. It was where we had met. When the phone rang, I was sitting in my mom's backyard, enjoying the afternoon. I have no idea why I picked up, because the call was from a number I didn't recognize. I wouldn't even consider picking up the phone from an unknown number today. Believe me when I say that. When I heard Teddy's familiar voice, my head started swimming. Was it really him? We hadn't spoken for so many years.

In order to understand the next part of this story, we need to back up to the beginning.

The fact that Teddy and I met in rehab probably should have been the only red flag I needed, but I was young and dumb and didn't know how drug addicts functioned. After all, I wasn't one. When my mother sent me to rehab at fifteen, I had never done a drug.

So, Teddy and I did not have drug use in common, but we did happen to be from the same town and enrolled in the same high school. We learned that during our six blissful rehab weeks together. I hadn't been aware that Teddy went to my school before then because I'd just moved to that town. Apparently, Teddy and I were in the same English class. I remember this because for many years, he reminded me that he used to check out my butt in that class.

During rehab, our romance was fairly innocent. Nothing major happened. It wasn't until we were sent back home that we started getting more intimate. This was another thing that Teddy liked to remind me about throughout the years. He'd like to mention how long it had been since the first time we slept together and then tell me about his specific memories, which always made me blush.

Teddy made me feel loved. That's probably the most important thing to know about him. I knew my family loved me, too, but my home life felt confusing in a lot of ways. With Teddy, there was no confusion. He thought I was a queen. The way he treated me in the beginning made me feel better about myself, and like I had someone I could count on.

But Teddy was a troublemaker. After we got back to high school, he kept abusing drugs. He wasn't into anything too hard-core at that point, but he did like to get high whenever he could. Eventually, his parents, who felt they could no longer control their son, sent him to military school in Norfolk, Virginia.

Teddy and I wrote each other long letters after that. It was incredibly romantic. And it was also sad, because he'd been forced to move to a different state. During this period, I started thinking of him as the one who got away. I loved him so much. I didn't understand how such deep love was possible before Teddy. Still, we didn't remain in a committed relationship, because it didn't make sense to do that. We were so many miles away from each other. In the back of my mind, even at that young age, I was probably imagining a future in which we built a life together. I really thought he was perfect, and every time somebody would refer to us as Ken and Barbie, I'd smile.

I met Teddy in 1989. From 1990 to 1992, he was in military school in Virginia. Then, in 1993, I went to college. Around this time, or maybe even slightly before, Teddy started going to jail for committing petty crimes. He was doing more drugs. He started to steal things. Sometimes, when I was on a break from school and Teddy wasn't in jail, we'd run into each other in our hometown, and I would be reminded of how much I loved Teddy. Every time I saw him, it was like time stopped. During these years, we'd get back together for the short periods we were both home, and then I'd lose track of him again.

In 1995, Teddy was sentenced to prison for the first time for uttering and publishing. He was basically trying to steal money to pay for drugs, and he received a sentence of four to twenty-eight years. He ended up spending four years in prison. From time to time, I would look him up online. Michigan keeps updated photos of its prisoners on the internet; they're not hard to find. It was weird, watching Teddy age in a series of prison photos from afar.

In 1999, Teddy was released. We reconnected, and this time our relationship was more serious than before. That summer, he invited me to his parents' beach house in the Outer Banks in Duck, North Carolina. I remember shopping for the perfect bikini to wear. His whole family would be going, which included his mom, his dad, his sister, his brother, and some friends. I was so nervous. I'd never been on vacation with a boyfriend before.

Technically, Teddy wasn't supposed to leave the state because he was on parole, so the trip felt risky to me. I've never been one to break the rules. But, if Teddy's family thought it was okay, then maybe it was?

They drove to North Carolina, and I flew out later to meet them. I was so anxious as I grabbed my luggage from the baggage claim area. I couldn't wait to see him. I still remember how elated I was when I saw him pull up in his blue Ford Explorer.

We started the drive to the Outer Banks. The tall trees along the freeway reminded me of my childhood in rural Michigan. The sun was shining. And Teddy was so cute, and his eyes were the most remarkable aqua-blue color. He was wearing a polo shirt and boat shoes. He liked preppy clothes, which I liked, too. I was wearing cut-offs, a tank top, and flip-flops. It already felt like the perfect summer.

At some point, not long into the drive, we pulled off the freeway and made love right there on the side of the road. It was exhilarating. I might have felt like I was in a movie about my own life. I still had no idea about how heroin affected the user, or that Teddy was heading back to being a full-blown addict by this time. He'd lost some weight, which I didn't even think to connect to heroin use. I also didn't know how, when he was using, his aqua-blue eyes appeared to be even more brilliantly beautiful.

Once we got to the beach house and I greeted all of his family members, I went upstairs to change—and realized that I had grabbed the wrong bag at the airport. That's how nervous I was. The next day, Teddy drove me back to exchange the bag I'd accidentally taken for the one that was mine. The rest of the trip was like a fairy tale. When I look back on our relationship now, I think that week in the Outer Banks might have been one of our very best.

For the next year or so, Teddy and I continued to see each other. I was working at the Detroit Auto Show. He didn't have a job, and he was still getting into trouble, but somehow I convinced myself that it was a phase. Later, when he grew up and came to his senses, everything would be okay.

One day in 2000, while I was at work, I got a call from Teddy's dad telling me that Teddy had gotten high on heroin, passed out while driving on the freeway, and crashed his car. I left work immediately and went to meet Teddy at the hospital. Thankfully, he wasn't seriously injured. My most vivid recollection of that day is how angry and rude Teddy was when he saw me.

"What's *she* doing here?" he asked as he walked feebly out of the hospital.

I took this personally at the time. I was naïve about drugs. Now I see that Teddy was just withdrawing from heroin, which is a painful process. That night, I was exposed to that process for the first time. I spent the night at Teddy's house, although neither of us really slept. Teddy kept waking up to vomit into the bucket he'd placed by the bed, and his poor body wouldn't stop shivering.

Teddy was on parole during the time of this accident, and the next day, after he'd started to feel better, I encouraged him to be honest with his parole agent.

"You need to tell him you had a relapse," I said. "And a car accident."

Honesty was not exactly Teddy's forte, but somehow, on that day, he decided to tell the truth. I drove him to his parole agent's office and waited outside while Teddy confessed. Afterward, the agent appeared and gave me the bad news.

"Sorry, but we have to take him." He handed me an envelope. Teddy's watch and wallet were inside. "These are his possessions."

I felt like my heart had been ripped out of my body. It was so excruciating to have to say goodbye.

For the next few months, I was living with my mom and step-father while I looked for my own place. I had my own personal phone line at their house. Every time he called me collect from prison, I accepted the call. Teddy was already proving how completely he could consume my life. Along with talking to him on the phone, I became very close with his mother during this period. We talked constantly, and of course it was always about Teddy.

Then I moved to California. At some point I wrote Teddy a letter saying that we needed to stop talking on the phone so much because I wouldn't be able to move on while having contact. It was a painful letter to write, but I knew it was the truth. He truly wasn't going anywhere in life, and I had to move on. We exchanged some letters afterward, and I still thought he was my one true love, and the one who had gotten away—again. Even when I was dating other men, the idea of Teddy and our potential as a couple was locked in the back of my mind.

After the parole agent sent Teddy back to prison, he was in there for fourteen years. When he got out, I was living my new life in California. Honestly, I think one of the reasons my mother pushed me to move to LA was to get away from him. Even his mother, who I was close to, thought I needed an escape.

In 2004, while I was living in Hermosa Beach, I received another phone call about Teddy.

This time, he said, "I robbed a bank."

CHAPTER 20

My Long-Lost Love?

The bank Teddy robbed was in a small, wealthy town. There was a massive search for him after it happened. The police found him running through a field. He thought about ending it right there, but then he told me that he pictured my face and knew he needed to surrender. He was crying hysterically as he told me this.

"I couldn't kill myself because I love you," he said.

I believed him. And I loved him, too. Even the fact that he'd been living in a hotel with a prostitute before he robbed the bank was unimportant when I measured it against our love.

Teddy was sentenced to ten to forty years. My close friend sent me an article about the bank robbery from the local paper in Detroit. Teddy's mug shot appeared along with a description of what he had done. It was heartbreaking and a lot to process.

More years passed. Teddy and I continued to write letters to each other for a while, and I stayed very close to his mom. Every time I went home for the holidays and during the summers, too, I'd see her. She used to give me the most extravagant Christmas gifts, for which I was always really grateful.

At some point, Teddy asked me to freeze my eggs. Meanwhile, all my friends were getting married and having children and living regular lives—or at least lives in which they weren't dating bank robbers who wanted their eggs frozen. I realized that if I wanted to move on with my life, I had to cut off contact with Teddy. It was so painful to do that, but I managed to sever the connection.

For years after that, I kept in touch with his mother, but then I realized that relationship had to be severed as well. We had one thing in common: Teddy. And so all we did was talk about Teddy, how we hoped Teddy would change, and how badly Teddy had messed up his life. Right before I got the job at the Cecil was when I stopped talking to his mom. I cared deeply for his family. It was difficult to make the cut, but I knew I was hanging on by talking to them.

As more years ticked by, I dated other people. I've mentioned Clive in this book, and there were other, less serious boyfriends, too, like Matteo, who I also mentioned briefly. I was so busy with work, though, that it was hard to maintain relationships. In a way, I think I was dating the Cecil for the ten years I worked there. For the most part, I had no contact with Teddy or his mom.

Now, flashing forward to June 7, 2018: my phone rang.

Again, the call was from a number I didn't recognize, and again, for whatever reason (kismet, I thought at the time), I picked it up.

"Amy," Teddy said, "I just got out of prison."

Teddy went on to tell me that he'd been released the day before after spending fourteen long years incarcerated. He said that he had my number written down on a piece of paper and kept it in his pocket for years. When he pulled it out, he hesitated before calling me. He wasn't sure if I'd be happy to hear from him or not.

I didn't know how I felt, honestly. I was happy and scared at the same time. I also couldn't believe the coincidence. What were the chances? And what were the chances that Teddy, too, was in Michigan, staying in a hotel with his parents? They'd moved to the Carolinas after he'd gone to prison, but had returned to pick him up when he was released.

"Will you come meet me?" he asked.

I went to meet him the very next day.

CHAPTER 21

Ups and Downs

Two months later, on August 8, 2018, Teddy and I got married.

According to the photos of the wedding, we were embarking on a fantastic life. The ceremony took place at Meadow Brook Hall, which is a mansion originally owned by the Dodge family. For that day, we forgot about all the bad times and focused only on what was good. Teddy had changed in prison. He was going to be a perfect citizen from now on. And all of our history meant—well, it meant that we were destined to be married.

A couple of weeks after our marriage, Teddy had a major surgery in Michigan. He was honest about his drug background at the beginning. I flew in to be there. He had severe complications and with the next round of doctors he wasn't so honest about his history. He was prescribed painkillers in the hospital after the operation—and this triggered his drug addiction. When he took more than the prescribed amount the first time, he was honest with me about it. When he did it the second time, he lied to me about it. And just like that, Teddy was back to his old ways, but I wasn't quite ready to admit it yet even though I knew that something was off and he wasn't himself.

I flew to Michigan to visit him, and then I went back to California. I had to work. He had to heal. The plan was for him to move to LA to be with me after he healed, but then his wound got infected, so he had to stay in Michigan for a while. He ended up moving in with my closest friend at the time while he was allegedly getting healthier. And while he was staying there, he stole prescription pills and a bunch of other things from her house. This later led to the dissolution of that friendship, which is a shame. It still haunts me. I was so lost in it all.

Obviously, his relapses made me very concerned about our future, but because I'd just married this man in a fairy-tale wedding, with the idea that we were destined to be together, I remained hopeful. Love does crazy things to your brain, and if you don't understand how addiction really works, you can stay in denial for a very long time.

In October 2018, Teddy finally recuperated from his surgery. He flew to LA. By this point, he was already an active drug addict again. He'd stolen my friend's daughter's Adderall, which put him in a terrible mood. He was mean to me. It reminded me of the time I'd gone to meet him at the hospital after his heroin-induced car accident and he'd said, "What is *she* doing here?"

Shortly after Teddy had moved into my apartment in LA, a friend of mine was over and he hit her. That's when things really took a turn. I left the apartment, and then later, after he apologized, I went back. One night, he beat my ten-pound dog, Maverick. I took Maverick to the hospital and learned that he had broken ribs and a torn trachea. I spent thousands of dollars on surgeries to fix him.

In short, my life turned into a total disaster very, very fast. And meanwhile I had so much work to do. My interior design business was thriving. My clients needed me.

It took the destruction of my life to show me that I'd been living the dream before Teddy reentered the picture. I'd been making tons of money, traveling the world, continuing to create jewelry, and enjoying my total independence.

And now I was coming to terms with the fact that I'd made a terrible mistake.

On top of the violence and the drug use, there was the humiliation. Teddy and I had gone to high school together. We knew the same people. On our wedding day, I posted a picture of us at the mansion on Facebook with a caption that said: *This is the happiest day of my life.*

All my life, I had wanted to get married and have a baby. In reality, I'd spent years feeling isolated and losing myself in work to combat the isolation. I'd also spent years dating the wrong people. I thought Teddy was going to be the answer to all of my dreams.

Before Teddy moved to California, a parole agent had to come to my house and make notes about it. While that happened, I was thinking, *This isn't going to be a problem. He's done his time.*

Here's a question I never asked:

What's Teddy going to do for work?

Why did I never ask that question? Because I'd decided instead that I'd support us both. So, while I worked around the clock, trying to meet all my clients' needs (while pretending that everything was okay at home), Teddy was getting sicker and sicker. One day, right before I was about to head off to a job, he jumped into the back of my car and said, "I'm going to kill myself."

I was so in fear of being judged that I didn't tell anyone about this, or about his drug use.

And (again, this is the insanity of love) I still kind of thought he deserved a second chance.

But then, not long after Teddy arrived in LA, he was living in a Motel 6 on Sunset.

On April 1, 2019, I filed for a restraining order and a divorce.

But I continued to see Teddy anyway. The neighbors knew what was going on with us because of the screaming they'd heard. If they saw Teddy, they would have called the police. So I left the door open for him at night so he could sneak in. That's how twisted my heart and mind had become. Nothing made sense. I knew I needed to get away from him, but I couldn't. I had gone back to Michigan to remodel my grandmother's house over the summer, and I'd gotten a generous check for doing so. I decided the only way I could escape Teddy was to leave. I packed up everything I owned, loaded up my dogs, Goose and Maverick, and drove back alone. I hoped that if I didn't see him for a while, I would get some clarity.

CHAPTER 22

The TV Show

Being back in Michigan was bleak. My dogs hated it. They didn't understand what snow was. I didn't understand how I was going to move forward with my life. I felt stuck. If I returned to California, I was probably going to keep seeing Teddy, even though I knew he was violent and dangerous. If I stayed in Michigan, well, was that a good idea?

Then, on January 13, 2020, I got an email from Netflix.

I had always wanted to tell the real story of the Cecil, and Netflix, according to their email, wanted to do the same thing. I thought it was perfect timing. What else was I doing but hanging out in Michigan, being sad and alone? I felt lost. I am a shy person for the most part. I think they caught me at the right time.

Elisa Lam was mentioned in the initial email, but I definitely didn't get the impression that she was going to be the central character of the documentary. I thought it was about the hotel in general.

Yes, I assumed that the horrors of the Cecil's past would be sensationalized, as they always were, and I thought this would be my chance to correct the hotel's reputation, or at least to broaden it. The Cecil was not only a place where bad things happened. It was a place where real people, like me, worked. Also, there had been a lot of misinformation that came out about Elisa Lam and the hotel after she died. I thought that participating in the documentary would be my chance to state the truth.

So I said yes.

I was told that I would be paid $1,500 and that my interviews would begin in Los Angeles in February 2020.

Shortly after agreeing to do the documentary, I decided that I would not be returning to Los Angeles to live. Even though there were a lot of questions and reasons I didn't want to return to my past, I did. I had to physically remove myself from California if I ever wanted to get away from Teddy. He just had this power over me, and I became powerless in his grasp. My friend Faith agreed to move into my apartment as a subletter for a while. And at the end of January 2020, I drove to Michigan in a moving truck.

When it came time to do the interviews, I flew back to LA, packed up all my stuff, and hired movers to drive my belongings to Michigan. I drove myself separately with Goose and Maverick. On the way, I made a pit stop at the Tucson gem show, which I try to attend every year. A few days later, I arrived in Michigan—but my stuff never did. The movers never delivered it. My material life had evaporated.

This meant that when it was time to go back to LA for the Netflix interview, I didn't have any clothes to wear, except for what was in a small bag I'd packed. The rest of my stuff would be there in five to ten business days. I called my friend in Michigan who happened to have a professional shopper, and we went to the mall together. I told her that I was going to be in a documentary, and she picked an outfit for me.

Even though Netflix barely paid me, they did treat me like a star, at least momentarily. They flew me back out to LA, they put me up in a hotel, and on the day of the interview, they sent a limousine to pick me up. My hairdresser, Susan, came with me. I had been seeing her for almost twenty years at that point, and she'd said she would do my hair and makeup.

The interview took place over the course of a single day. We started early in the morning and ended at nighttime. It was exhausting. I remember getting a tip from a friend beforehand to put Vaseline on my lips because I'd be talking a lot. There was a lot of probing, and the questions were intense. I hadn't prepared for any of it and was equally unprepared for what it all meant. We had only a very few short breaks. I could barely move my lips afterward; they felt like sandpaper. It was also overwhelming. I'd never been on camera before, and I didn't understand how daunting it was to be flooded in all that lighting. I was very grateful that Susan stayed the entire time, not only because she made me look better, but more important, because she was the one person on that set who I felt that I could trust.

The questions I was asked were about all sorts of things that had happened at the Cecil. It was still by no means clear that the docuseries would end up being primarily focused on Elisa Lam. I tried to be as honest as possible, and at certain points, I got emotional. I remember crying really hard. They cut that part. I wish that they hadn't, because maybe if people had seen it, they wouldn't have thought of me as an emotionless robot. The way things are edited matters.

The two Cecil employees interviewed were Santiago and me. I'd asked Santiago and a bunch of others if they wanted to participate, but Santiago was the only one who said yes. I found a translator for him. He was paid very little, and it ended up being emotionally taxing for him to recount the day he found Elisa Lam's body in the water tank. I regret involving him.

The day of the interview was the first time Susan had ever heard about the real details of my old job. I didn't tell most people, because I assumed they wouldn't understand.

"Wow," she said, after listening for a while, "these stories are incredible."

It was nice to get that validation, and I thought that it boded well for the future. Perhaps viewers would come to see that there was more to the Cecil than just Richard Ramirez and Elisa Lam.

While I was back in LA for the interview, I did not see Teddy, although through text and phone calls he claimed that he'd been to rehab, which turned out to be a lie. He hadn't gotten a job, because his parents were still sending him money. Instead of working, he bought drugs and did them in sad motel rooms or random Airbnb rentals.

"What are you doing all day?" I asked him.

"I don't know," he said, "but I miss you."

Shortly after this call, I called his parents and told them that they were essentially killing Teddy by continuing to fund his habit.

When Teddy found out about this, he threatened to tell my land-lord that I had an illegal subletter. Sometimes the most horrible moments are not the ones that break the camel's back. Teddy beat my dog. I continued to struggle on a dangerous roller coaster with someone I loved and was very sick. I broke up with him when it became clear to me that he was willing to see me lose my home. That's when I realized that Teddy cared more about drugs than he cared about me, and there was nothing I could do to change that.

So, finally, I stopped speaking to him.

CHAPTER 23

Lockdown

After the Netflix interview was over, I was back in Michigan with some cash I'd saved and a plan to continue my interior design business. Coming from LA, I thought it would be easy to get clients. I was paying very little in rent. I thought I had plenty of time. Since my possessions had never arrived from LA (I later sued the moving company and won), I slept on an air mattress that would deflate every night on a hardwood floor. I was still half waiting for my things to appear, so I didn't want to invest in new furniture yet. Many nights, as I drifted off to sleep, I wondered how the hell I had gone from a fairy-tale wedding to an air mattress on a Michigan floor. It made me feel even more compassionate toward the tenants at the Cecil, many of whom were contending with tumultuous circumstances.

I tried to stick to a routine and not get depressed. Soon, a new plan would present itself, I thought. Then, a month later, Covid hit, and everybody's plans were altered.

I continued to dress my dogs in little coats throughout the rest of winter, and they continued to hate the snow. I realized I hated it, too. After twenty years of living in California, the cold was unbearable to me. Meanwhile, I hadn't been able to start up my business because of Covid, and I was more alone than ever.

In August 2020, I moved back to California. My subletter, Faith, had left my apartment in ruins. She hadn't taken the trash out once since she'd moved in.

"I know you're not well," I said, "because this does not make sense."

Faith was so depressed that she didn't even have the energy to move out. I helped her gather her things, and she left to live with her son. I never saw her again after that day. Six months later, she killed herself.

That August, I tried to start over. I cleaned my apartment from top to bottom. I repainted the walls. I would have tried to dive back into my interior design business, but because of Covid, there wasn't much in-person work I could do. I collected unemployment. I spent a lot of time thinking about the past, and a lot of time thinking about the future. I might have wanted to contact Teddy sometimes, but I never did. Months passed. Then more months. It was a very hard time for me—and for the rest of the world. Once in a while, I'd mention to someone that I'd done this interview for Netflix, but that was rare because I was spending so much time alone. When I thought about the upcoming series, I felt anxious. What would it be like? How would the Cecil be portrayed? How would I be portrayed?

In January 2021, about a year after I'd been interviewed, I got a call from the producer, a woman with whom I'd been friendly. I really liked her. Mostly, we communicated via text or email, but this time, she asked me if I had time for a call. I thought that seemed a little bit ominous, or at least out of the ordinary.

Once we got on the phone, she said, "Amy, I wanted to talk to you before the series airs." She then told me that it would be best to watch all of the episodes before forming an opinion. Near the end, she said, the intentions of the series would become more clear. But before that, there were most likely going to be parts that would throw me off. "After you're done watching it, though," she said, "I think you're going to like it."

I assumed this meant that Netflix had edited my interviews for dramatic effect, but by "edited," I guess I was thinking they'd just cut me off early sometimes. I definitely never thought my words would be taken out of context and placed in new contexts, which gave them new meaning. Basically, I thought the editing process was going to be linear, not a patchwork job.

One week before the show aired, I was given an access code so I could watch it early. I invited my hairdresser, Susan, over for a viewing party. It was bizarre to see myself on a screen. I felt judgmental of my appearance, which I think is common. Sweet Susan, who is such a supportive friend (and a great hairdresser), kept telling me I looked beautiful, which was nice. In certain moments, I felt proud of what I'd said. When I had been asked what I hoped for the Cecil, my answer was, "I wish the Cecil peace." It was one of those things that I meant from the bottom of my heart, and it was conveyed in exactly the way I had meant it.

Other things I said did not fall into this category. I was aware of that the first time I watched. When a part was taken out of context, I remembered how the producer had said, "You might feel thrown off." I did feel thrown off. But I was glad that nothing had been misconstrued to the point of a potential lawsuit. After all these years, because of my job at the Cecil, I still think about things in legal terms. I didn't think any of Netflix's editing was going to cast me as somehow culpable, and I was relieved about that much at least.

Overall, I was content enough after the first time I watched the show. Susan and I watched the entire thing in one sitting. I'd had no idea that it was going to be four hours long, or that I was going to get so much airtime.

I also had no idea that a body double was going to represent me. There are close-up shots of a blond woman applying bright red lipstick, and of a woman's heels as she walks down a hallway. Both of these are how Netflix chose to show the viewer that I enjoyed dressing up for work, I suppose. I was fine with the lipstick shots. I even thought they were kind of funny. The footage of the woman walking, however, was disturbing to me, because her heels were so ugly, and she was wearing nylons. Nylons! The hideousness of these choices became a joke between me and the producer. Basically, I said, "How could you do this to me?" Later, when she told me that Netflix had sent me a gift, I asked if it was new shoes. (It turned out to be a poster.)

The main surprise, beyond the body double's attire and the fact that I was kind of the star of the documentary, was its focus on Elisa Lam. I understood why Netflix had chosen to do that. The case garnered tons of press, first of all, and second of all, there were all the conspiracy theories surrounding her death. Even years later, people on the internet were discussing it at length. This probably should have been a clue about what was to come. Who sits at their computer years after a horrific death and continues to espouse theories about how it happened?

Obsessive people.

The day I saw the show for the first time, I wasn't really thinking about that. I was just taking it all in with Susan.

"You're wonderful, Amy," she kept saying, "and you look so good."

There was one moment, though, when Susan's support turned to worry. Did the way in which Netflix juxtaposed slices of my interview with footage of the hotel kind of suggest that I was sketchy? Susan thought so.

I'll never forget the moment she turned to me and said, "Amy, people are going to watch this and think you murdered Elisa Lam." I didn't believe her at first. I had already been through so much, and was it possible that my experiences at the Cecil weren't over?

CHAPTER 24

Representing the Cecil

During the week leading up to the public release of *Crime Scene: The Vanishing at the Cecil Hotel*, I was asked to do a series of interviews. If I had known then how my life was about to be picked apart by tons of strangers on the internet, I probably would have declined. But since I had no idea about what was to come, I said yes.

It was a grueling week. Some of the interviews were being conducted by people in different time zones, which meant that in certain cases, I had to get up very early in the morning. Netflix gave me a list of talking points to consider before the week began:

You must have crazy stories. Tell us about your time with Cecil. How do you normalize working at a place where you saw more than eighty deaths in your time, and countless other criminal activities?

The series focuses heavily on Elisa Lam's disappearance. What was it like being in the hotel then? How did it change the Cecil? What are your hopes for the hotel in the future? Do you ever go back to the hotel?

Some people think there's a dark force lurking at the Cecil. What makes it a magnet for strange and tragic occurrences?

I was also given a list of Dos and Don'ts. Here are some examples: *Assume the microphone and camera are always on. Take control of your interview. Don't fill silences, repeat the negative, or get political.*

Basically, it was a crash course in public speaking. I found the week just as overwhelming as the day we shot the show. That's what I was most concerned with at the time: how uncomfortable I felt, and how determined I was to push past that discomfort with the goal of changing the way the public thought about the Cecil.

Because of Covid, the press junket took place on Zoom. I drove to Susan's house early every morning so that she could do my hair. Again, it was such an isolating time, and I was very grateful for her support—and for her clarity. After one of the news outlets asked me about the Elisa Lam elevator footage in a way that seemed to suggest that maybe I had tampered with it, she said, "See? They are making it sound like you had something to do with her death."

This made me extremely uneasy, but what was I supposed to do about it? All I could do was keep going and keep telling the truth.

I did interviews for print, TV, and radio. This might seem odd, but when I was asked about what it was like to work in a place where people were dying all the time, it actually gave me pause. I hadn't categorized the Cecil as the place where people went to die. I mean, that might have been part of it, but to me, that wasn't the distinguishing characteristic of the hotel. It was a business, and I was in charge of running it. That was a big thing I wanted to convey: how seriously I took my job, and how much I cared about the people who lived, stayed, and worked at the Cecil.

Could I succeed in conveying that to the public? Or were the darkest facts about the Cecil the only thing people cared about?

During the week of press, I felt hopeful that viewers would have room to understand the hotel not just as one thing, but as many things.

Then, in February 2021, the show aired, and I quickly learned what it was like to be very misunderstood.

CHAPTER 25

The Reaction

No amount of preparation could have readied me for the public's reaction to the show.

Right after it was released, I received an onslaught of text messages from friends and family, some of whom I hadn't seen or spoken to in many years. All of them were impressed, I think, that I had ended up on TV at all.

Awesome job on Netflix!

I received a version of this message dozens of times, and of course it was nice to get the encouragement. I felt less scared about the future, too. Maybe everyone would be nice?

Obviously, that was a naïve ideal. After the text messages, I started getting contacted on social media. I had a Facebook account with about six hundred friends, and I had just set up an Instagram business account for my jewelry business. Before the show aired, I had gained some followers on Instagram that were genuinely interested in jewelry.

Then, a day or two later, the tide turned. My Instagram inbox got flooded with thousands of messages, which ran the gamut from nice to unnecessarily malicious. On the nice end of the spectrum, there were the viewers who wrote things like, "I love you, Amy Price!" In the middle of the spectrum, there were the messages about the nylons that belonged to the body double, which of course people assumed was me. Bizarrely, some of those seemed to verge on fetishism. I found that unsettling, and surprising. I hadn't known there were so many nylon fans out there. I seriously don't wear them and think they are awful. And then, on the malicious end of the spectrum, there were all the strangers who hurt my feelings. They criticized my appearance and the way I spoke. Many said that I appeared to have no emotion. Some thought my lack of emotion was a side effect of too much Botox. Others thought I should have done more for Elisa Lam. She'd exhibited signs of mental illness before she disappeared, and I had been aware of that, and therefore, it was my duty to . . . I don't know what they expected me to have done, honestly. Dial 911?

Those messages were very hard to read. So were the ones that accused me of tampering with video footage, and of killing Elisa Lam. How could anyone possibly have thought I would be capable of doing that? Anyone that actually knows me understands that I am far from techy.

I became so overwhelmed that I ended up giving Susan's daughter my account information and asking her to delete the mean comments. I switched back and forth between a private profile to a public one so many times. I wanted people to be able to see my jewelry, but not to tell me about the reasons they hated me. Even the producers of the show reached out and apologized for all the abusive comments that were coming my way.

I couldn't let Susan's daughter manage my account forever, so eventually, I took over again. The mean comments kept coming. I received death threats. One stranger told me they were going to hunt me down and kill me and my family. I have a small family. We are close. The first time this happened, I tried not to take it seriously, but then it kept happening. It got to the point where I started fearing for my life. The hardest part was that there was really no solution. The best I could do was delete the comments, block problematic accounts, and keep moving.

Was I glad when the show hit number one and stayed there for weeks? Yes and no. Of course I was thrilled that the hotel was getting attention, and of course I was upset that a lot of it was negative. The people who were close to me tried to say the right things.

"Don't pay attention!"

"Who cares what random strangers on the internet are saying about you? They don't know you!"

"Sticks and stones!"

While I could see the good intentions behind this cheerleading, I still felt lonely. It's hard to understand what it's like to receive so much negativity unless it's happened to you. I think it would have been hard for anyone at any time, but it's worth pointing out that I was in a vulnerable position already. Between Teddy and Covid, the previous few years had been brutal. How was I feeling about myself? Not great. My point is that when you get mean comments online that mirror the mean comments in your head, it's even more difficult.

In the docuseries, there is a storyline about a man named Morbid that reflects my experience of being negatively impacted by conspiracy theorists online. Our similarities actually get even more specific than that. Morbid, too, has been blamed for Elisa Lam's death.

Coincidentally, he happened to be staying at the hotel when she died, and his appearance looks as morbid as his name, which many web sleuths interpreted to mean "murderer." Morbid's intentions, meanwhile, seem to be more aligned with Alice Cooper's. His ghoulish costume is about art, not actual death.

In the series, Morbid recounts the dark turn his life took after the web sleuths started harassing him. For a time, he considered killing himself. He also thought about giving up his music career completely and moving on to some other medium, one that would allow him to inhabit a new, less potentially offensive character.

In the docuseries, Morbid is depicted with total compassion. Any viewer with a heart would have felt sorry for him, and probably defensive, too. What those mean online comments did to his self-esteem was devastating.

After those same mean comments started pouring into my inbox, I related to Morbid. I also thought it was deeply ironic that same show that had been so sensitive to his plight would incite the same plight for me. The only difference was that mine would take place privately.

At least I had Pedro. His enthusiasm about me being on TV was hilariously over the top. After he watched the show, he called me and said, "Oh my god, Price! You're a movie star!"

It warmed my heart to see him so happy, and I didn't want to ruin that, so instead of telling him about how all the negativity was ruining my peace, I just said, "Thanks, Pedro." Sometimes it's better to bask in the glow of somebody else's happiness than it is to dive deeper into your own despair.

Sadness wasn't the only thing I felt, though. I was angry, too. How could people treat me so badly? And how could they treat the Cecil so badly? When the other talking heads in the documentary were asked about why they thought so many bad things had happened there and they responded with statements like, "Well, it's just a dark, bad place, right next to Skid Row," it pissed me off. I thought, *How is this the Cecil's fault? What has she ever done to anyone?* Blaming the Cecil for its location was like blaming the *Titanic* for being located near that iceberg.

After the show came out, I felt protective of my cherished hotel, and I felt more protective of myself. I had trusted these filmmakers to tell my story, but I'd made the mistake of assuming that we understood my story in the same way. It's amazing to me how, despite all the shady characters I've encountered in my life, I continue to want to see the best in people. It's this quality that allowed me to stay at the Cecil for so long. I really do believe that we are all doing our best.

Along with all the negatives that came from the documentary, there were many positives, too. I've received countless lovely messages from fans. A woman who owns a hotel told me she felt moved by how much I cared about the hotel. A handful of men have asked me out on dates. (I haven't said yes to any of them yet.) Random strangers send me compliments. That's always nice.

When people recognize me out on the street, I find it funny. A person will stare at me for a beat, then say, "Do I know you?" Or they'll get it immediately. "You're the manager of that hotel!" I would be lying if I didn't say that it's always bizarre to me when it clicks with people who know who I am. After it all, it was the craziest job I hope I ever have.

Another positive: jewelry sales. Right after the show came out, I received an influx of orders. Since my passion for jewelry is the most important thing to me, all the positive feedback has been incredibly bolstering. It's still not easy for me to put my art out there, but I'm doing it anyway.

I suppose the increased curiosity of the press about me and my private life has been intriguing for the most part. My friend sent me an article at some point that said, "Where is Amy Price Now?" I was glad nobody dug up the dirt on me and Teddy. That was a big fear of mine.

Teddy, speaking of which, showed up at my apartment after the show aired and screamed my name repeatedly. He also left flowers and food. I still haven't responded to him.

This brings me to the biggest way in which the show made my life better: it made me a stronger person. After I got through the period of horrible insecurity, of second-guessing every choice I made, and of thinking all the mean comments online were true, I emerged as a more complete self. I grew a thicker skin. I learned to trust my own thoughts over the thoughts of other people. This has not been quick or an easy road. I am still learning, and I am still healing.

CHAPTER 26

The True Meaning of Love

The Cecil Hotel in Downtown Los Angeles, California, is not famous because of its near one-hundred-year history or its beautiful Beaux-Arts lobby, but rather because it has been the scene of tragedies and deaths many times over. It was popularly called "America's Hotel Death," according to *Esquire*.

The hotel has undergone many revamps throughout the years, but it reopened in December 2021, repurposed as low-income housing: Hotel Cecil Apartments in partnership with the Skid Row Housing Trust.

Through "adaptive reuse"—a process that helps repurpose a building at costs much lower than creating a new building—the Cecil Hotel was able to renovate for $75 million instead of $300 million, according to *LAist*.

On December 14, 2021, Cecil Hotel Apartments opened.

The six hundred units range between 160 and 175 square feet, and the common areas include bathrooms and kitchens, which is similar to the hotel's earlier days. It also offers guarded entry and case management services on-site.

The rooms are exclusively available to rent by low-income Los Angelenos who earn between 30 and 60 percent of the area's median income of $24,850 annually. With rent ranging between $900 and $1,200 a month, tenants can use Section 8 housing vouchers to help pay.

This excerpt from a 2022 Insider.com article about the Cecil paints an apt picture of how its function has transformed. Will this change its reputation over time? Or will the Cecil always be known as the place where the girl died in the water tank and where Richard Ramirez slept?

I don't know how the Cecil will be remembered by society, but here's how I will remember it:

I will remember it as the place that taught me to see homeless people as not that far removed from everybody else. No child thinks, *I am going to be homeless.* No child thinks they're going to end up in an alley prostituting themselves for the price of a McDonald's Happy Meal. Nobody plans to scurry around the streets of LA talking to themselves. Nobody plans to sleep naked on the street.

I will remember the Cecil as the place where I learned that everybody has a story, and that the determining factor of whether that story is mostly happy or mostly sad is really nothing more than luck.

The Cecil taught me that people have secrets, some bigger than others, and that almost all of us deal with shame.

I will remember the employees at the Cecil, specifically the ones who sacrificed everything to immigrate to this country. I'll remember how happy they were to do the shittiest jobs.

Mostly, I will remember the Cecil as the place that taught me the true meaning of friendship, and of love.

CHAPTER 27

A Beautiful Disaster

Recently, I went to pick up Pedro for lunch.

When I got off the freeway and started driving down the familiar streets of downtown LA, it looked the same as it always has, with some improvements. It's funny how much more civilized the blocks that contain the government buildings have become. The grass is always just a little bit greener on those blocks. Of course, there are still homeless people everywhere.

I arrived ten minutes early. I parked across the street from the Cecil and gazed up. It's incredible how dark the building feels these days. I'm sure there are many reasons that contribute to that feeling of darkness. The exterior of the building is dirtier than usual; the old marquee is gone. In front of where the hotel restaurant was going to be, a homeless woman was doing her own version of yoga. I couldn't tell if she was high, mentally ill, or both. There were people out front taking pictures. I assumed they knew it from the documentary, and I thought that if I got out of the car, they might recognize me.

On my side of the street, there was the familiar dry cleaner that I used to go to once a week. A homeless man was passed out right in front. I watched him to see if I could detect any movement. I couldn't.

Right at noon, Pedro emerged from the main doors. He's easy to notice because he's always wearing that familiar work uniform. The reason it's familiar to me is because I chose that uniform back in the day. When Pedro saw me, his face lit up, and then he jogged across the street and got into the car.

"Price!" he said.

"Pedro!"

Together, we watched a man open the door to the Stay lobby. I'd never seen him before. "That's the manager," Pedro said. It felt funny that somebody else, somebody I didn't even know, would be called the manager of the building.

On the short drive to the salad place, I started to fill Pedro in on the latest with my mom's health. He said something he's said before, which is that it's crazy that American families don't continue to live together. White people count down the days until their children leave. Hispanic people never want their kids to leave! When my mom first moved to California, he suggested that we move in together. I thought he was insane.

At the restaurant, I ordered for him and for myself. We know each other so well I always order for the both of us regardless of where we are. We sat outside in the sun and he told me about how his grandsons are doing now. They're still potty training, but soon, they'll learn how to go by themselves. Kids grow up so fast.

Our conversation meandered over to the subject of the hotel. I asked him if they'd corrected the rat problem he'd mentioned to me recently. He said yes, although there were so many rats that it wouldn't be surprising to find out that the exterminator had missed a few.

"How many rats?" I asked him.

"At least a hundred," he said in his funny voice.

"Only in the basement?"

"No, in the lobby, too. Julio killed at least two of them with his broom."

"Pedro! Weren't you terrified?"

"No."

"What about the tenants?" I asked. "Are there any updates?"

Pedro told me that a man I knew from the old days had been found dead in his truck. He'd died of natural causes. I was happy to hear that his son had come to collect his belongings. I didn't even know he'd had a son. Apparently, the son didn't leave with anything, though. He took one look at the stuff and said, "Junk."

"Sounds familiar," I said, and Pedro agreed.

After lunch, I drove him back to the hotel, and promised him that in a few weeks, we'd do it again.

"Bye, Price," he said.

"Bye, Pedro."

I said *I love you* in Spanish like I had heard in the Taco Bell commercial many years before.

"Te quiero."

And then I watched him walk across the street, thinking about how you really never know who is going to enter your life and change you forever. I had arrived at the Hotel Cecil with plans to do a three-day design job. Over a decade later, there I was, watching my best friend glide through the lobby doors, tireless as ever.

I was sad not to be joining him, but then again, was I?

Sometimes I don't know if I should cry because my time at the Cecil is over or laugh because it happened. The whole experience was a beautiful disaster.

The Front Desk Archives

During my time at the Cecil, I received dozens and dozens of notes from employees working at the front desk. I saved many of them. Unless otherwise indicated, all of these notes were written by front desk agents or security guards. Some have been edited for concision.

2009 / Naked Guy

This [a photocopy of his license was included] is the guy who was found naked and shivering in the men's dorm last week. He was the same guy who had taken the mattresses off all of the beds and basically trashed the room. He booked a reservation online through open hospitality and tried to check in last night. I went ahead and cancelled his reservation, declined him service, told him that he no longer was allowed to stay at the hotel. I also went ahead and put him on the hotel "blacklist."

2014 / Deceased

At about noon on Sunday, an investigator came to the lobby with two LAPD officers. Apparently, a registered guest had taken his own life a block away from the property. When they found the guest, they found his room key in his pocket (room 704).

2014 / Fire Escape Artist

Around midnight during a routine walk around the property, security found a hotel guest on the fire escape. He was given a warning. At about 2:30am I received a call from a business across the street expressing a concern that there might be someone on our roof. Security was given the key to investigate. On the roof he found a hotel guest alone with art materials, including pens, markers, paints, a sketch pad, etc. Security asked him to leave.

2015 / DAMN

Mr. Tyler, who is a resident in 309 came in with six of his friends this morning wanting to take them up to his room. Now I wasn't sure what the rules were in this situation, because some rules that are put in place for the guests don't apply to the residents. For instance, Mr. Mike Mayley smells like the world's biggest ashtray, and smokes in his room like cigarettes are going out of style even though smoking isn't allowed for guests.

So anyway, Mr. Tyler from 309 [came] to the front desk and [said he wanted] to take his friends up to his room. By this time, it was just him and two girls. I told him that I would need to take their IDs in order for them to go up. And then he said he wanted to bring up even more people.

Usually, Mr. Tyler stutters when he talks, but this time he was clearly wasted and he kept going on and on about how he was famous and wanted to have his "fans" come visit him in his room for a while. He said he had just finished a concert on Sunset Blvd., with his very famous cover band . . . (apparently they're world famous).

Seriously, can't even tell you how many times he told me he was famous. So I let the girls go up, after they left their IDs, but then I got a call from Dolores in 308 saying the girls were on the fire escape. I have to admit I was kind of glad, because I got to kick them out.

Security went up to the room and made sure the girls left the property . . . but then two of his male friends took their place. DAMN.

2015 / Sex on the Roof

Two guests checked into room 1307. At around 12:30am, they began making jokes about the Elisa Lam incident. Shortly after that, the guests in 1308 began calling. They stated that someone was on the fire escape. Security went to investigate but didn't find anyone. Then security checked the roof and found the guests from 1307 engaging in sexual intercourse near the water tank. They were escorted off the premises and advised there would be no refund.

APPENDIX

2015 / Not Leaving / Police Delay

Our guest in room 1143 was caught going up on the roof at
4:40pm. When this was discovered, we asked them to leave due
to breaking hotel policy. They did not. They went back to their
room and stayed there. We called the police, but they didn't show
up until 9:30pm.

2015 / Indecent Exposure

Hello. At around 10:50pm I received a call from our neighbors
across the street stating they saw someone on the fire escape on
the ninth floor, so they took out their binoculars and what they
saw wasn't appropriate.

Apparently, the man was doing indecent exposure. He was
wearing a hat and dark sunglasses. I immediately asked security
to go up and check. The guard came back to the desk and said it
was Mr. Lawrence. I wasn't able to talk to Mr. Lawrence, because
according to the guard he looked like he was "out of it."

2015 / Ejected

A man and a woman checked into room 534. A friend of theirs,
who assured me he would not be staying, was helping them with
luggage/equipment. I saw that the equipment included a tripod.
I told them to stay off the roof just in case. The woman assured
me that they had no intention of going there as she's afraid of
heights.

A few minutes later, security saw someone with a tripod getting into the elevator. I called room 534 and there was no answer.

Security went to the roof. The two gentlemen were both on the roof and the woman was on the fire escape. They were escorted to their room to get their belongings and ejected from the hotel.

2016 / A Crack Pipe and a Liquor Bottle Under the Bed

This morning, Christopher Amir Lopez came to the front desk to report (complain) about the cleaning service of the room. After the cleaning, his wife noticed a crack pipe and a liquor bottle under the bed. Because of that, he had a huge argument with his wife. He alleged that those items do not belong to him and were left over from the previous guest. He doesn't want any compensation or refund. He just wants us to call his wife and explain this confusion. Her number is 323-XXX-XXX. He doesn't want to lose his marriage or his child, who is coming soon. (His wife is pregnant.)

2015 / Four Female Loiterers and a Man Who Forgot What Happened Last Night

At 5pm, I noticed two women loiterers enter the hotel lobby. I reported it to security. They reported back to me that the women had gone to room 1302, where there were two other women along with the male guest who had paid for the room. The hotel policy [about occupancy] was explained to the guest, but he refused to comply. Because the group would not vacate the room, we called the police.

It turns out one of the women had a $30,000 warrant. She was handcuffed and arrested. The other women and the man were also removed and added to the blacklist. All four women showed symptoms of recent narcotic use.

According to the night auditor, the guest returned to the lobby at 5am, disoriented and weary. He wanted to know what had happened the night before and if he himself had been at the hotel.

2016 / "I am going to stab the ear that god talked to."

Today at about 11am when there was a really long line for check-outs, and a guy came into the lobby and started talking really loudly and vulgarly to a guest. He was an Asian man with glasses and didn't look homeless or anything, so at first I thought he was a guest talking to another guest.

However, it quickly became obvious that the man was not normal. He started interacting with other guests in a weird, uncomfortable way. He was ranting and raving and mentioned being suicidal at least twice. After security could not convince him to leave I called the police. When I informed the man the police were coming he took the pen from off the front desk, brought it next to his head, and said, "I am going to stab the ear that god talked to."

He was absolutely insane. After a few more minutes, he

finally walked outside with security following close behind, and hasn't been back since.

The police never even showed up, so I'm filing an incident report, but everyone just keep an eye out for this lunatic, because he might come back. Asian guy, glasses, wearing a black t-shirt with red polo logo and blue/gray jeans.

2016 / Stephanie Brown

Stephanie Brown was asked to leave the premises due to her extremely disruptive and rude behavior. Throughout the night, Ms. Brown was acting very strange, going in and out of the women's restroom in the lobby area.

About half an hour later, around 2:30am, Ms. Brown called the front desk and said that the outlets were not working. I asked her if she needed the maintenance man to go up to her room. She declined. Minutes later, she called again and said the outlets were still not working and asked me to send maintenance. They advised over the radio that the outlets were working fine, and that the problem was probably her charger.

The maintenance man came and advised me that when he entered Ms. Brown's room, she began to scream. Once in the room, he claimed Ms. Brown was being extremely rude and yelling at him about the outlets not working. Two guests from nearby rooms called and said they couldn't sleep because of the yelling.

Ms. Brown was told she needed to check out because of her behavior was disturbing other guests. She refused and I notified LAPD.

APPENDIX

2016 / Jumper

At about 9:30pm, LAPD came to arrest Mr. Jason Johns in room 429 because his brother called them saying that he was trying to jump from the fire escape. According to the police, he was taken to have a mental evaluation. All his property is still in the room.

2016 / $100

At 10pm, a houseman informed me that security was investigating an incident in Darren Lawrence's room. Mr. Lawrence's reported that a man named Bryan, the nephew of an acquaintance, had come to his door and demanded to be given $100. Mr. Lawrence denied owing Bryan money and asked him to leave. Bryan kicked the door repeatedly and also scratched it. Mr. Lawrence yelled for help. Another resident informed security. Bryan has facial tattoos, a bike, and was wearing a hoodie.

2016 / "I was airing myself out."

Around 10:20pm, the guest in room 1146 said that she'd been listening to a man yelling for the past hour. I went with security to that hallway and heard nothing, but I did find a bag of beer bottles and a pair of underwear on the fire escape.

On a hunch we went to the roof and there was a man standing at the far end naked. He said, "You caught me. I was airing myself out."

2016 / Suicide Attempt

Police arrived unannounced at 7:55pm saying that they had gotten a call from room 343 about a suicide attempt. I took them to the room and knocked.

A woman named Sharon answered. She said that her friend, Ms. Heart, was in the bathroom. Apparently, Ms. Heart had taken a handful of pills, then involuntarily thrown them up in the toilet.

Sharon also said that Ms. Heart suffered from PTSD. The police separated the women. Sharon gave details while Ms. Heart sat on the bed handcuffed for everyone's safety. LAPD had a difficult time getting details from Ms. Heart as she was quite belligerent.

At 8:30pm, Los Angeles Fire Department/LAFD arrived and Ms. Heart was taken by gurney, still handcuffed and not speaking.

Ms. Heart is blacklisted due to her attempt to commit suicide last night.

Acknowledgments

To my family. I love you so much. Thank you for putting up with me.

To every single person who worked at the Cecil and Stay on Main. You all gave me so much. Because of you, I am closer to understanding what sacrifice means. This is something I will take with me for the rest of my life. I wish you all peace. You deserve it.

Thank you, Susan, for taking the action that was necessary for Netflix. I seriously had no idea what that all really meant at the time and what it would mean after. Thank you for being there for me. You taught me countless things about friendship.

To my sweet circle of friends who supported me in this process. You are all warriors in your own way. I love that about each and every one of you. As much as you heard me, I want you to know that I hear and see you, too. I LOVE YOU AND I MEAN IT.

To Mauro DiPreta and Liz Parker. Thank you for making this happen.

To Swan Huntley. Thank you for being so easy to work with.

ACKNOWLEDGMENTS

To all the places I have been. Each place has taught me something worth learning and I can't wait to learn more.

In loving memory of Faith Taylor. You will always be a bright light in my life, and I will never forget you.

To my loving dad in heaven. Even though you never had the chance to get there, you were always with me. I love you.